Praise for *From Hippos*

CW00523275

Leaders cannot help but be provoked by this bo[ok ...] will make their first leap for the future. *Hippos* [...] small or evolutionary changes are no longer enou[gh ...] keep pace or to continue to be relevant. Leaping from a Hippo to a Gazelle in a single generation is what is called for.
Cliff Burrows, President of US Operations, Starbucks Coffee Company, Seattle

Every leader at the top of a corporation struggles with how to get the organisation to realize its full potential, how to get it to excel at the discipline of getting things done. This book vividly demonstrates how, if you can get alignment and 'create' more leaders in your organisation who all want to take the corporation to the same place – it is easier. Why are answers to difficult challenges often so simple?
Mark Garrett, Chief Executive, Borealis, Vienna

The authors pull you into their world and – without theorising – take us through the warts-and-all journey of a real change situation. This is a refreshing insight into the tricky business of change and the leadership that can make it happen. Woven into the narrative are helpful references to academics and business thinkers so that we are able to learn as we witness the events of the merger unfurl.
Alison Young, Director of Management Development, Pearson plc

Highly recommended for people leading change. Philip Goodwin and Tony Page take us on a leadership safari through Africa. Through their vibrant stories, they emphasise engagement – 'the feeling agenda', weaving patterns and paths for leaders in organisations. Their personal journey and reflections are invaluable, vividly showing the commitment and courage of people – creating new leaders, listening deeply, generating new patterns, leaders transforming themselves.
Dr Monica Sharma, Director of Leadership and Capacity Development, United Nations

An insightful and warm engaging book into the fundamentals to change management, in terms of results, people and respect.
Esa Saarinen, Finnish Philosopher and Professor at Helsinki University of Technology

This engaging and refreshing book has much to offer leaders at all levels, as well as the business graduate and professionals interested in leadership and change. Drawing on a fable set in Africa, a meta-story unfolds to reveal real life characters, their feelings, anxieties, hopes and aspirations, and builds into a transformation. This shows that the leadership and change issues faced in that continent are similar to those faced elsewhere in the world.
Dr Ann Shacklady-Smith, Senior Fellow, Manchester Business School

A refreshing and insightful guide to organisational leadership and change, advocating a thoughtful and people-centred way of achieving high performance. The combination of using fables and the African context is … fabulous.

Alan Coppin, Chair of Redstone plc and Patron of Windsor Leadership Trust

I fully endorse the approach in this book. This tremendously colourful contribution challenges the reader to lead in the way that makes it most enjoyable and rewarding for everyone. Not every leader will agree at first with the notion that everyone else can be a leader. However the authors have spotted the need in today's conditions for leadership to be gripped less tightly at the top of a hierarchy and much more widely shared amongst the workforce. I found this approach gave me the feeling that the people who worked in my organisation were a life-raft, supporting me rather than holding me back. Of course people have different aspirations; not everyone wants to be a leader at every stage of their career. But where the leader can make people feel that a brick which was on their head has been placed under their feet, the increased momentum is tremendous.

Dame Sue Street DCB, former Permanent Secretary, UK Department of Culture, Media and Sport, British Government

For those seeking to lead fundamental change in their organisation, this handbook, firmly grounded in the best organisational practices – and with a light touch – provides an inspirational and comprehensive guide.

Jamie Hamilton, Head of Market Fundamentals, BG Group

The successful management of change is critical to any forward thinking business which has aspirations of growth and development. This book demonstrates real insight and presents the ideas in a fresh and innovative manner – definitely worth a read.

John Philip, Vice President for London, Hilton Hotels Corporation

This is a really useful book which takes the reader through the practical steps of a true account of achieving a successful merger and change programme, told through the experiences of the leader, the facilitator and various participants. The imaginative mix of stories, shared experiences, the approaches used, key theories and effective tools combine to provide an excellent practical pathway which is recommended to anyone involved with this most challenging of issues.

Alan Hooper, Founder of the Centre for Leadership Studies, University of Exeter

This book will encourage a debate on how leadership *at all levels* can be developed. The chief executive of today and tomorrow is essentially a 'leader of leaders'. Here is a stimulating case study … within an African context to build an effective strategic leadership team, and in the process to change old-style managers into inspirational leaders – hippos into gazelles.

John Adair, internationally acknowledged authority on leadership

From Hippos to Gazelles

How leaders create leaders

Philip Goodwin
Tony Page

 Kingsham Press

www.akdpress.com

First published in 2008
by Kingsham Press and British Council

Kingsham Press
Oldbury Complex
Marsh Lane
Easthampnett
Chichester, West Sussex
PO18 0JW
United Kingdom

British Council
10 Spring Gardens
London SW1A 2BN
United Kingdom

Typeset in Minion

Printed and bound in the UK by Biddles Ltd., Kings Lynn, Norfolk

ISBN: 978-1-904235-45-3

British Library Cataloging in Publication Data
A catalogue record of this book is available from the British Library

Goodwin, Philip; Page, Tony

The story that follows is a true account of events taking place during a merger and change programme seen through the eyes of a leader and facilitator. Some names and places have been changed to protect the anonymity of the people involved.

Contents

Part 3: The Path

Part 1

The Challenge

1

If leadership were logical…

The fable of the people who turned into hippos, lions and gazelles

The people in the villages worked hard. Each season brought fresh rains to water their crops and they became well-fed and prosperous, but with each passing year they became sleepier with their success.

One year the rains failed and the crops did not grow tall but people carried on as before, saying, *"we have stored enough grain"*. When the following year the same thing happened, their stocks became low. *"Things will return to normal next year"*, they said to each other, *"Just you wait and see"*.

Something surprising was happening in the sub-Saharan Africa operation, but at first it was not obvious. Everyone was so used to this part of the world being a no-hoper languishing at the bottom of the company league tables, they did not notice the early signs of the tide beginning to turn. No-one expected investment here to deliver big results and since it was expensive to operate in such a volatile environment, this brought a constant demoralising threat of cuts. Then, the company promoted a young manager – Philip – and ordered him to merge two disparate regions – East and West. Against the odds, this merger was a success and as solid evidence of positive business results began to pile up, staff morale rose until their confidence in the leadership hit a staggering 74% positive, beating the best performing public and private sector organisations in the UK.

Noticing this two years after the merger, people in headquarters started asking why this was happening. At first, Philip and Tony found it hard to explain and this was frustrating as they were bursting to share what they had learned. Finally, they hit on the idea of telling the story as a fable (see above).

And as the fable continued to its conclusion, people became interested. They said *"Yes, that's a real campfire story and very entertaining. But what is it really telling us?"* Tony and Philip said, *"It is telling you what you can do as a leader to deliver sustainable business results and ensure your merger or change programme will succeed. But we understand that at first, this may not seem obvious because, if leadership were logical, we would have no story to tell".*

When three years before, Philip presented to 30 senior managers a well-argued case for merging their two organisations, logically they should have been bowled over and not wasted a further minute in implementing the strategy presented. People in headquarters would have vigorously applauded and copied the lessons across the world. But this isn't what happened. Why not?

A decision which appears logical to you as a leader and beneficial to the organisation as a whole, arrives for each individual as if out of nowhere. Your clarity arises out of a defining moment when as leader, you realise things must change – whether to cut losses, increase profit, gain market share, increase impact or maintain the relevance of your organisation. In practice, strategic decisions are always taken by a few and affect the lives of many.

In this case, the leader had to achieve a fundamental shift in delivery, killing off hundreds of well-loved, local products for a handful of big cross-regional blockbusters. Offices had to close. New teams and reporting lines had to be created. All of this would affect around 500 staff across East and West Africa.

This story is about the delivery of hard business results and given that there are 500 staff in this business, there are likely to be 500 different stories of how this happened. But the story we choose to tell in this book is the "multiplier" story – about how one leader engages 30 leaders who engage their 500 staff of different nationalities, cultures and allegiances spread across 11 countries and thousands of miles. We think this story of aligning and engaging staff, unleashing their energy to achieve lasting change, is the real work of a leader. Otim, one of our African senior managers, describes the ethos like this:

"The leadership style is about believing people have the potential. If you can find that button which you need to push, then their potential comes out to the full… It doesn't matter what grade you are in the organisation or what level, you have a contribution to make".

Yes, we are offering you a fable but don't get confused. This is real life and not some fairy-tale myth. As our story unravels, you'll see that the notion of a leader as a knight on a white charger deploying a mixture of charisma, authority and brute logic is narrow, mistaken and long out of date. Rarely do we need leaders who operate unilaterally. Conducting a merger of different cultures be they corporate, national or tribal in this fast moving but fragile world, requires a new form of leadership that spreads out to others and releases the hidden capacities in people.

Our story is set in Africa and reflects issues that exist in any merger or change programme. We will describe a specific interplay between leader and led which must happen anywhere before a change programme delivers a positive outcome that can be sustained over time.

Merging and changing are everyday matters in organisational life today – in every sector and in all parts of the world. Worryingly though, the evidence indicates that between half and two-thirds of all mergers fail to deliver the value required (Bieshaar et al, McKinsey, 2001) and similar failure rates have been stated for other corporate programmes to restructure, introduce change or implement new strategy. Our story addresses this problem. In a nutshell, our proposition is this:

Leaders create leaders

If you are a leader who wants to avoid getting trapped in a repeating yo-yo of poorly executed change programmes which drive people crazy and drain their energy, then this is for you. In this book, you will find out how to help people grip the controls they need to adapt, continuously, swiftly, collaboratively and with much less pain. In doing so, you will create an organisation that is committed, confident and capable of delivering improved performance.

This book is about sparking motivation in others and about you finding your true work as a leader. It is about leaders creating leaders and ultimately about what must happen in all our organisations and society at large, if we are to find the courage to survive the most difficult and frightening challenges facing us today.

Read on ….

2 Preparing for change

Fable Part 2

The villages in the East were different than those in the West and their people rarely met because they were separated by a great desert. Each had their own customs and ways of seeing the world but both claimed their warriors were more skilful and their wine more delicious than the others.

The East and the West assumed they had little in common. They exaggerated their differences saying "we are all like this" and "they are all like that". In fact, each side included diverse people from many tribes and traditions: some friendly others formal; some quiet others pushy; some compliant, others dominant, and so on.

In fact, East and West were less different than they thought but since they didn't believe they had a problem, they had no interest in finding out what they had in common, or how they could help one another, or indeed in working with the other side in any way at all.

When Tony and Philip first met in a wet and rainy London, Philip's organisation had just embarked on a new global strategy. His Executive Board had given him the task of leading the merger of the East and West Africa business units to form a new integrated region. Why? As with many organisations, the world around them is moving so rapidly that holding on to the old ways of doing business constantly threatens to make them an expensive irrelevance.

Faced with such change, organisations can carry on as before and perhaps even get away with it for a few more years, but with each year that passes it becomes less likely that they will ever be able to catch up.

In practice, Philip's Executive Board had decided to grip the challenges it faced across the globe by decentralising activities into 13 regions, each of which would have a Regional Director charged with achieving synergies of cost and impact. Whilst there are many stories of success we could tell from different parts of the world, in the story that follows we put the spotlight on just one region, Philip's, as an example of a business entity undergoing a merger and change. For simplicity and clarity, we will refer to this region as "the organisation".

As one of their newly appointed Regional Directors, the Board had given Philip a sense of urgency and indicated the scale of transformation required. He wanted to move quickly in merging his East and West Africa teams, to get them operational as quickly as possible. To do that, he needed a business vision and a plan for delivering it. He wanted them to put themselves at the forefront of a wave of change rolling across the global organisation, otherwise he feared they could all too easily become victims of it.

So newly promoted and eager to move at once, Philip decided to call his new senior managers together. Yes, he was bright-eyed and keen but he wasn't naïve about what he was taking on. He would be working with a wide range of experienced executives who between them had seen it all. How would his arrival be received?

Previously, Philip had been based in East Africa. Would his West African colleagues be resentful or suspicious? He knew there might be resistance to change. He knew there were likely to be multiple agendas in the room. How could he possibly see all these agendas? How would he bring them into the open? How would he get people to engage with each other as a team? How would he bring alignment between the different team members?

He wanted a facilitator to share the heat and got Tony's name from a colleague who had read Tony's book "*Diary of a Change Agent*". Philip was drawn to the reflective approach described in the book which chimed with his own belief that the immediate business gains following mergers and change can only be sustained if at the same time you work towards long-term culture change. Tony brought Ben Parker, a colleague from his consultancy network, to the meeting. They struck Philip as a good combination: Tony using questions to draw you out, coaching you to explore and grip the issues, while Ben was the "hard man", more in your face, wanting to clear a path through the jungle.

For Tony, the project in Africa contained the familiar challenges of leadership and engagement during a complex programme of change, but set in a totally unfamiliar and multi-cultural context. While excited by this, he was also wary not to get blinded by Philip's obvious enthusiasm. He asked Philip what outcomes were needed and Philip almost too quickly replied:

"At the end of three days, I want a shared vision and an agreed transition plan".

So Tony pushed him to articulate what he really intended to happen longer term and Philip gave a response which surprised and inspired Tony:

"I've learned that real success only arrives if you can push leadership down so that people take responsibility, joining up in teams to address their common problems and what I really want is to release the creativity and intelligence of all 500 people in my business".

Suddenly to Tony this made a lot of sense: he felt excited and willing to invest energy in taking it on. As they explored Philip's vision further it became plain how ambitious it was. The current reality was 500 people physically divided across 11 different countries, split between East and West Africa. Typically working in isolated offices of around 40 staff, people knew and cared very little about the merger. Mostly African, many were doing routine, relatively low paid jobs, their instructions passed down through a hierarchical chain of command from an expatriate UK Country Director. Each country had a different culture although most shared a colonial legacy that still strongly influenced feelings and behaviour.

Philip was troubled by a "feed me" attitude, even amongst quite senior people, who failed to deliver on promises, avoided responsibility and passed problems back up the line. He wanted a high performance culture and knew that this required a fundamental transformation of attitudes and behaviour. When Tony asked Philip how he intended to release the intelligence of 500 staff, Philip said:

"We will begin by bringing together 30 leaders".

What in effect we were seeking to do was create an aligned leadership community although, at the start, we did not know how the 30 leaders would carry forward the merger with the wider staff of 500.

Philip's initial questions about engaging the leadership community were:

- Who are the most important people to have in the initial group of 30?
- How do I bring the opportunity to them?
- How much thinking and planning do we do before it is time to get on with it?
- How do we balance the need to deliver results with the need to change?

Tony and Ben, both experienced members of a consulting network (which assists executive boards and leadership teams to engage people during business-driven change), shared with Philip their knowledge of three agendas originally set out more than 2000 years ago by Aristotle (Marlier and Parker, 2008) and that leaders need to embrace:

- The strategic "thinking" agenda
- The behavioural "doing" agenda
- The engagement "feeling" agenda.

Typically, the leader begins in blind enthusiasm, thinking like a Finance or Logistics Director: What is the business case? What are the logics, benefits and costs? What are the big tasks and when do we need to do them by? What level of performance do we need to attain?

It is quite right that leaders address the **Thinking Agenda**, because it is their job to set out the rationale and the pathway for moving forward. However this tends to unleash a tsunami of activity, called the **Doing Agenda**, in an urgent effort to operationalise the merger. There are suddenly pressing demands on each person in the organisation to produce plans, objectives, budgets, campaigns, logo, signage, systems, structures, job descriptions, responsibilities, resourcing, skills, rewards, incentives, and management processes. Phew! With this swirl of internal activity, it is not surprising that corporate performance and motivation take a hit.

What the leader is in danger of missing is their key role in transforming the emotions of their team. A leader attuned to the **Feeling Agenda** slows down, and starts to think and behave differently. They understand how change can damage a person's ego, identity and life-support system. They know the "logic of emotion" and make themselves aware of what people are feeling: on the one hand containing the fear and on the other, tapping into courage, passion, creativity and positive excitement. This is called being emotionally intelligent.

How do they do this? They engage people through their behaviour. Specifically the leader shares vital information about why change is happening. This often brings people a harsh dose of reality. The leader asks useful questions then shuts up and listens to the words and feelings coming back. The leader challenges and supports people to digest the difficult new reality and address the real choices before them. They inspire and strengthen people with relevant stories and powerful behavioural signals. Just like Philip intended, they seek to push problem-solving down and step back to enable others to fill the leadership space.

All three of us came out of our London meeting energised and with the courage to embark together on something quite challenging. We recognised that in spite of all our experience and good intentions, we were taking a big step into the unknown and, we recognised that we needed to expect surprises. We agreed to conduct frequent reviews, learn lessons from what happened in practice and be prepared to keep adjusting our roles and priorities.

The story that follows is a tale of what it takes for a leader to align 500 people after a merger. The difficulties you expect in any merger are amplified here both because of the distance and because of the specific cultural legacy with its strong hierarchical flavours of dominance and subservience.

The story is told in five phases: each time the leadership team, but with several members changed, gathers in a different hotel in an African city, then disperses a few days later in aeroplanes to distant countries. Many months pass before we come back together, so on arrival everyone needs to retell the story-so-far to pick up the threads. It is like pressing a pause button on the change process. This has allowed us to capture quite a complex story of change, slowing it down to reveal the essential details. We now realise the five phases represent key shifts in leadership emphasis which are needed to drive engagement and deliver high performance. A pathway through the five phases is provided as an overview in a diagram (overleaf).

There are many voices in the story: Philip's, Tony's and those of several participants in the change programme. In each phase, we give you a similar, recognisable structure. One of us – Philip or Tony – begins with the key **challenge** of that phase and tells **our story** supported by the voices of other participants. The remaining sections of the chapter are from both the authors, except where we specifically indicate Philip or Tony's voice. Under **How do you approach this phase?** we share key theories, principles and ideas which shaped our approach and which will help you understand the **signs of progress** which follow. We then give you the **tools** that we used and **evidence of completing this phase**. Each chapter ends with a visual aide-memoire and some **tips** to support your work as a leader.

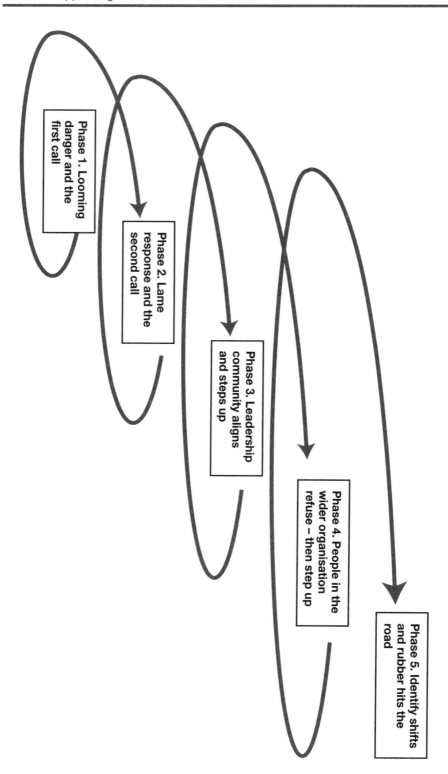

Phase 1. Looming danger and the first call

Phase 2. Lame response and the second call

Phase 3. Leadership community aligns and steps up

Phase 4. People in the wider organisation refuse – then step up

Phase 5. Identify shifts and rubber hits the road

Part 2

The Story

3 First phase: *Looming danger and making the first call …*

Fable Part 3

The sleepy people were blind to the looming danger that a brave young chief saw clearly. The first thing the young chief did was to call all the Chiefs from East and West together. He told them

"The rains are changing. We must combine the skills and resources of East and West and face this together. If we do not adapt, we are storing up great problems for ourselves that may threaten our very existence".

But the Chiefs did not believe him. Unafraid and fierce like a lion, the young chief waved his stick at them but like old male hippos – big, thick-skinned and sedentary – the other Chiefs were hard to rouse. The young chief didn't give up. He continued to provoke and prod the old chiefs. Then, irritated and tired of the young chief, and slightly in fear of him, the other Chiefs suddenly turned on one another, not just East against West but indiscriminately, and the young chief looked on with disbelief.

Finally, after much bellowing and baring of teeth, a single plan was agreed and the young chief went away exhausted, believing he had settled the matter and had called the Chiefs to action.

The Challenge

You know what has to be done and there's no time to be wasted. You bring people together and tell them *"This is important. We're under threat and we've got to move quickly if we're going to survive"* but the tragedy is they don't get it. It's as if you are in a dream. The building is on fire but no one gives a damn. You're shouting *"move, move, get out"* … but no one hears you. Or they hear you, stand up slowly and just sit down again.

Philip: Our story

It's a beautiful day outside in Nairobi. The sun is shining on the lake in front of the hotel. Behind the lake, some tourists are finishing a round of golf. There's a soft breeze blowing through the open windows of our meeting room. It's the sort of day when you feel content with life. My East and West Africa leadership team has come together in Kenya which has long been a tourist destination for Europeans and North Americans keen to experience its wonderful combination of beautiful and varied landscapes, amazing and abundant wildlife and its superb beaches gazing out on to the Indian Ocean. The service culture here in hotels and restaurants is excellent: not only do they defy "western" perceptions of how Africa *can* deliver, it also defies other Africans' expectations.

The group listen politely as I'm speaking. The coffee break is due in an hour and my team settle deeper into their chairs. Why worry when it's clear just by looking outside that all is well with the world?

But here I am explaining the challenges facing our organisation: trying to paint as vivid a picture as I can, trying to make it real, simple and inspiring! I have the task of leading the merger between the East and West Africa operations. This is a promotion for me. It's my first strategic leadership role and I'm meeting my new team for the first time all in one room. I'm a little nervous and I've been up early, practising what I want to say.

I've got to deliver a significant change programme and there's some urgency to getting this done. Yes, Tony and Ben have made me aware of the different agendas (thinking, doing, feeling) that an effective leader has to address with their team and I have the intention of addressing this. But the truth is I'm predominantly in "doing" or trouble-shooter mode, impatient and ready to push people hard to make the change. What needs to be done is clear to me and I anxiously want to galvanise people into action. With hind-sight it's perhaps a little too early to be like this when I haven't even yet met everyone!

I knew I would face a big challenge around the culture of this team. Historically, the management style had been somewhat hierarchical and paternalistic. This was a legacy of the African colonial past but also of an historical tendency towards a bureaucratic and civil service style within the organisation in which individual responsibility and initiative were limited because management "looks after" the team. Ian, a UK appointed country director from West Africa reflected how he and his colleagues were not particularly eager to change:

"There was a kind of lateral grumbling with colleagues. It was quite difficult to envisage what the benefits would be… it seemed local autonomy was being taken away, and to put it crudely, money would be taken away from us and allocated to regional activity that would be kind of homogenised and not entirely relevant to us here".

In calling the group together, my first step was to widen the pool of people that make up my new leadership team. 10 out of 11 of the heads of country operations in my team were from the UK, nine of them were men. To get a wider set of champions for change across the organisation, I invited 11 African senior managers – one from each of the business units – to join the leadership group. This was a first: the leadership team was now half UK, half African and a third of the leadership positions were taken by women.

For me, this was a watershed moment, a screaming headline of intent. It's as though I have been sitting round a campfire in the warmth trying to tell a story but outside the circle there were people I couldn't even see in the darkness but I knew they were there. I ask the circle to widen and invite those unseen faces to come nearer, to get warm and to hear what I have to say. I wanted to draw more people close to me as a leader. I wanted to send a clear message:

"We need wider involvement in strategic decision-making down the organisation. We need African voice in this team and I want to hear and respond to that voice".

This seemed to strike a chord with the African team members right from the start although Binte from Senegal in West Africa, was not expecting it:

"When I was asked to attend that workshop it was a shock and I wondered why me but I took the challenge because, in the past it was like I was in the shadows but being called into the leadership team, I was into the merger throughout and because of that I didn't find it a problem".

Fatima from Sudan was uneasy but at the same time, eager to see what change would bring:

"I was nervous because we didn't know what regionalisation would mean for us. West Africa was definitely a stranger but I was also excited because to me it would bring new opportunities, new faces and new things to learn".

Otim from Kenya in East Africa could already see practical benefits to the organisation from widening the circle:

"Having African senior managers in the group meant that we demystified the Leadership Team Meeting because for staff back in country it was much harder to believe UK Country Directors. Some staff are suspicious of UK management and say "yes, right! Like you tell us everything!" But if the messages come from an African senior manager, well that helped improve things. It meant a lot more dialogue so everyone knew what was going on".

But Otim was not yet convinced about the plans to regionalise:

"There was talk about people being given power or more control at regional level as opposed to in the UK. There were all these things going through my head but I wasn't too sure. There was a bit of 'yes we need decisions to be made faster' but also 'will this really happen?'"

As this new group arrived in Nairobi, I enjoyed my first experience of bringing together people from across Africa. Strangely, it is often easier for African professionals to travel to Europe or to North America than to other African countries particularly across the East-West African route. Many of our African team had never travelled to each others' countries before and there was a real delight in discovering new things about their continent and meeting fellow Africans in their home countries.

The question we set out to answer at this meeting was: *How will this merger produce synergies: greater impact and relevance at lower cost?* We had a three day programme of intensive work to answer this. The venue is great, the mood is good but our luck doesn't hold, Ben goes down with flu and can hardly stand. We're already one man down before we've started!

As the meeting begins, I quickly pick up an underlying cynicism from the group as though they are thinking:

"Leaders come and go, as will their ideas. What makes this new guy any different? We'll simply ride this one out".

In this comfortable environment, without the pressures of the day job, you can almost hear individuals thinking

"What really matters is not these abstract corporate concerns but what I'm doing in my country operation. We'll do a bit of talking here and then I'll go back and get on with the real work".

As Ian, one of the Country Directors, said:

"If I'm honest, looking back we shrugged our shoulders and said we'd get on with what we were already doing".

Tony, Ben and I guessed right that most of the senior managers present – let alone the other 470 people who worked in the organisation across East and West Africa – knew and cared very little about the new region, OR about the new corporate strategy, OR the coming financial squeeze, OR the changing context which was giving rise to it. As Akello from a provincial office in Sierra Leone said:

"I was saying to myself 'is the organisation really serious or are they just going with the fads....there's probably all new management and they want to show off that they've come up with another beautiful idea!'".

As the three days progressed, we moved through a process of setting out the challenge, getting to know who we were in the room and where we were as a team, before starting to set out a transition plan that would help us move from where we were now to meeting the new challenges.

The initial sense of pleasure and excitement soon turned to struggle. Yahya, a senior manager from Ghana in West Africa, noticed how people had different perspectives on the merger:

"It was like the case of six blind men touching an elephant and describing the elephant by the parts that they touch".

Time kept running out because people were unable to let go of their concerns and wanted to return again and again to the issues. We asked the group to prioritise the challenges facing us and when the exercise was almost complete someone piped up, *"but what about issue number 17? Isn't that important?"* and the group started again, dancing round the issue, exhausting each other but not moving forward. As Tony observed:

"This group could literally talk for Britain! And they hated decisions! They say they are 'inclusive' but they're poor at listening, stifling others – particularly subordinates – and they can be brutal in doing so, railroading those who don't agree with them".

Ultimately, no-one wanted a final decision about anything because that would mean letting go.

At the start of the meeting the new African members of the leadership team had been positively surprised:

"This is a workshop that is dealing with real issues of strategic importance and you want our input!"

But after several sessions when the UK heads of operation still dominated and were in many respects, territorial, like hippos fighting – everyone else gets out of the way – the pressure was building up. On the final day a dramatic moment arrived when Fatima had had enough:

"I actually stood and said 'I feel we, the local members of staff, are not participating fully and I don't see the point of attending if we are not given the opportunity to talk freely and to be heard'. There was quite a big silence in the room!"

This divided the group into those who under time pressure, felt it important to push on and get a result, and those who said it was important to pause and address Fatima's point. Facing this impasse, Tony and Ben instructed each table to conduct a review of how people felt about the progress we were making and how the behaviour of group members was contributing or not to that progress. They were asked to listen briefly to each person in turn without responding (see Tools below, *Five Minute Process Review*) before continuing the work. This intervention recovered the meeting, allowing us to move forward.

In concrete terms, after much pushing, prodding and coaxing along, we did finally produce a preliminary deal on funding the new region, a vision of what change would deliver for us and a twelve month transition plan to deliver the merger as I had hoped. By the end, Fatima's smile had returned:

"This meeting really changed the vision I had of our organisation. Before we used to receive emails about the strategy but going to this meeting, ideas were brainstormed and decisions were made about how we would be working in the future. It really opened my eyes!"

Akello who had been struggling to identify how working regionally could benefit her local office, had begun to find some answers:

"It was really beautiful to see everybody talking about what fears they had. It was a kind of a motivation for me that the concerns I had were shared by many other people and that we could overcome those fears by focussing on the same

vision. Yes, it was really comforting and encouraging. But the concerns did not go away immediately. There was still that extra mile of deciding who were the people who were going to take this forward".

After the huge pressure to get a result many people clearly felt tired, rushed and browbeaten. I had been huffing impatiently around the meeting and at the time, I thought *"Thank God! At least we've produced a plan. If we can go away and deliver this at least we'll be on our way!"*

However, although the team *had* produced the transition plan themselves and *had* seemed to sign up to it, looking back there was a sense of *"Heh, we've done our bit"* and if you listened carefully you could hear an underlying air of: *"We know we have to merge. Okay. But how, as far as possible, can we get through this without changing anything?"* Looking back, Gabriel, a country director from Senegal, commented:

"There was a core group that felt, 'you know we've been down this road before and we will adopt the same methods that we adopted then...and it will go away'".

As we drove away from the meeting, I suddenly had this niggling doubt. Yes, we had the big plan but with all the pushing and shoving to come to a conclusion in the meeting, who now would actually take the actions? My fear was that it would be me and a few immediate colleagues.

So did we really get these people leading the merger? No! Were we really waking them up? No! When I got back to my desk the next week, I couldn't forget the moment when one of our heads of operations had simply said *"I don't see what the big deal is here".* It was clear the team didn't yet appreciate the enormity of the change required.

■ How do you approach this phase?

We all know that starting well is crucial. Linking back to the fable (Part 3), Philip is in the leader attitude of the brave young chief who sees a looming danger and is unafraid to say so. He would naturally begin boldly like a lion but Tony and Ben were pointing out that, instead of scaring 30 people, if he would step back a bit, it might be easier to motivate others to think about the future and make a sensible plan.

Motivating people in a very challenging task

In mergers, the people affected do not choose to merge, but one day they come into work and find out what is being arranged for them, a bit like a forced marriage. In this story, the decision to merge the African regions was decided by senior managers at head office in the UK. The managers in Africa had no choice. Research has shown that fewer than 20% of employees are prepared to make changes their leaders want them to make (Janice Prochaska et al 2001). But if the conditions are right, a person can participate in changes imposed by others. So, under what conditions can people be persuaded to invest their energies?

It will be no surprise that a critical factor is helping people to find their motivation particularly when they are confronted by a very challenging task. We knew that Philip was expecting a lot from people. When you ask people to go on a long march, they are happier, suffer less stress and perform better if you keep them fully informed about why they are marching, how far they have gone and how far they still have to go. If the goal seems too difficult, they simply give up at the outset. People generally prefer to tackle a task in manageable chunks (Shlomo Bresnitz 1989). So, we began with a clear doable objective for the meeting: to produce a transition plan. This was essentially a map that would help us find the answers to our challenge.

Framing the challenge

How should you actually confront people with the issue? As leader, the ball was firmly in Philip's court: he had to "frame" the challenge for this group. Bill Torbert is a professor at the Carroll School of Management, Boston, with a worldwide reputation for improving the quality of leadership in firms such as Gillette, PriceWaterhouse-Coopers and Volvo. He describes "framing" as the first of four speech acts which a leader needs to master to be influential and powerful in action

> *"The leader too often assumes that others know and share the overall objective… Explicit framing is useful precisely because the assumption of a shared frame is frequently untrue. When people have to guess at the frame ("What's he getting at?") we frequently guess wrong and because the frame is veiled… we often impute negative, manipulative motives"* (Torbert, 2004, p 28).

By "framing" we mean explicitly stating what the purpose of meeting is, what the dilemma is that everyone has to resolve and what assumptions you think are shared or not shared (but need to be tested out loud). In short, you put your perspective as well as your understanding of the others' perspectives out onto the table for examination.

Breaking the ice

You need to quickly break the ice, building high levels of trust and confidence so that people willingly focus on the work to be done. Tony began by describing in a series of positive statements how people can work through change from feeling as though they are victims of that change to taking responsibility for moving it forward. He then invited people to tell each other about a time when they had successful experiences of working with someone from another country.

These techniques called "positive preface" and "success stories" are part of the method of "Appreciative Inquiry" developed by David Cooperrider (Cooperrider and Whitney, 2005) that builds trust quickly in any group particularly where people do not know one another, where their cultures and backgrounds are diverse or where there is suspicion. An example of a past success question is: "*Tell me about a time when you were...?*" A future success question begins: "*Imagine you fell asleep for two years and woke up to find this team was producing an astonishing performance. What sort of things would you see happening?*"

Getting down to work

As we found, it is particularly difficult to get a large group of people – who, like many senior managers, enjoy talking – to start thinking practically about the future and their role in it. Marvin Weisbord and Sandra Janoff (1995) have developed a large group engagement method called "Future Search". This is extremely useful when people responsible for the future of an organisation or community need to make a paradigm shift in their thinking and actions. Their conclusion, from extensive worldwide experience of such conferences, is that if you want to get a group of people to think about the **future** you first have to get them to think about the **past** and the present.

You divide the large group up into small, self-managing groups of eight seated on round tables and ask them to map personal, organisational and global past events on a large wallchart called a "timeline" which is then examined for patterns and insights. Weisbord and Janoff's key discovery was that if you ask participants to share their feelings, not just their thoughts, then they tend to shift quite quickly from "moaning" to "owning", and from "me" to "we". They have experimented with different ways of preventing breast-beating and finger-pointing and come back to two questions: What are you proudest of? What are you sorriest about?

Conducting effective conversations

During the meeting, we observed a lot of negative comments in the form of harsh criticism, sarcasm and cynicism, and not a lot of encouragement, support or appreciation in the conversations. How concerned should we be? Research undertaken by Marcial Losada (Losada and Heaphy, 2004) has shown that there are striking correlations between how people in a team interact with one another in business meetings and their team's performance. Losada and colleagues classified interactions in terms of positivity/negativity, inquiry/advocacy and others/self. They found high performance teams displayed dramatically more positive comment (five times more positive than negative), slightly more exploration of others' positions (rather than just making statements of their own position) and an equal exploration of issues external and internal to the organisation.

On this basis, we clearly had a long way to go!

■ What are the signs of progress in this phase?

1. When the leader has prepared by considering how to motivate, rather than just scare the group with the scale of the challenge (Prochaska/Breznitz).
2. When the organisational challenge is clearly and explicitly framed (Torbert).
3. When the ice has been broken, trust is growing and participants are building confidence in their capacity to handle change (Cooperrider).
4. When the group is divided into smaller working groups which are letting go of the past, in preparation for thinking about the future (Weisbord and Janoff).
5. When the conversations are monitored for positivity, inquiry and balance in order to identify the shifts in habits of talking which will accelerate individual adaptation and speed up decision-making (Losada).

■ What are the tools you can use?

In this first phase, the leader can benefit from tools which provide collaborative ways to address certain key questions including: *How do you engage the leaders? Where are we now? What does the future look like? What are the first steps?* Here are four tools that are useful in doing this.

No 1: Raising the issues – Six Thinking Hats

When a group is not ready to talk about the future you can begin with a tool called Six Thinking Hats (De Bono, 2000). This is a structured brainstorm in which you gather thoughts about "the company" using each thinking hat in turn:

1. The facts (cool white hat)
2. The feelings (hot red hat)
3. The risks (gloomy black hat)
4. The opportunities (sunny yellow hat)
5. The really wild ideas (creative green hat)
6. The conclusions (sky blue hat).

We used this tool to help people identify the challenges and opportunities facing the merged region.

No 2: Visioning – 5/1/3

There are better ways to envision the future than simple brainstorming. Visioning in its most powerful form opens different parts of the brain to those we generally rely on and creates memories of the future which are intentional pathways to focus and channel your energy. Here are the steps:

1. Participants close their eyes and imagine waking up in five years time, when the merger or forced change is complete and delivering real benefits to stakeholders including staff.
2. You read out a simple script that walks them through "a typical working day five years from now", asking them questions which cause them to notice many small but important changes in their workplace (what do you

see, feel, hear, taste and smell? what do you see when you look in the face of your customer or colleague? etc)

3. Finally lead participants back towards the present pausing at a 12 month point in the future and a 3 month point to "rearrange things" in a way that makes the five year future possible.
4. When participants open their eyes they are asked in silence to scribble down as much of their 5/1/3 vision as they can remember.

No 3: Transition planning

When, after the imagining phase, you need to make change practical with concrete next steps you can do the following to develop a transition plan:

1. Pair people up to compare their visions, and then write "post-its" capturing key points for display on wall-charts.
2. Small groups cluster the "post-its" for each of the three future visions (five years, one year and three months) and produce a short sentence in the present tense describing what is happening.
3. Small groups present the sentences to the whole group. The facilitator asks for reactions, and about the links from one vision to the next.
4. Go to the 5-year vision and say "if this is to be real, each cluster needs to become an area of work that is addressed now by this team".
5. Participants arrange themselves into workstream groups and decide the actions needed over the next 12 months. Their actions are posted quarter by quarter on a large wall-chart labelled "Transition Plan". Plenary discuss and refine the plan.

No 4: Five minute process review

Transition planning isn't easy and sub-groups can get stuck in disagreements or lose their energy. A problem in one group tends to spread and erodes the momentum of the large group. What can you do about this? You can use the five minute process review as a fast, self-administered medicine:

1. The chair of each group suspends discussion of the topic, setting aside five minutes for a review.

2. The chair asks each person round the table very briefly to report on how they are feeling about the progress and behaviour of group members while the others just listen without responding.
3. After all have spoken the chair asks for any ideas about how to behave differently to perform better as a group.
4. The chair invites all to make the necessary adjustments to their own behaviour.
5. Return to the topic.

■ What is the evidence of completing this phase?

- The leader may be tricked into believing others are engaged.
- Or the leader may feel frustrated or thwarted at the inability of the team to recognise or respond to the very real threat that they are facing. At this stage that is OK and normal!
- There has been some talking but no real doing yet. With the exception of a few individuals, the leadership community are largely standing back and united in trying to maintain the status quo.

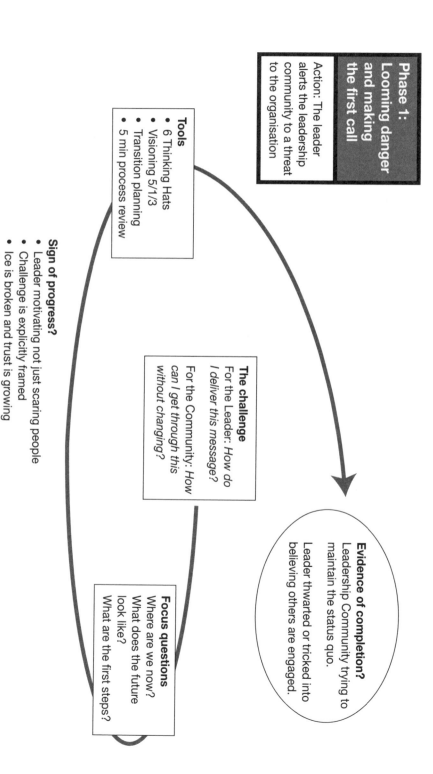

Phase 1: Looming danger and making the first call

Action: The leader alerts the leadership community to a threat to the organisation

Tools
- 6 Thinking Hats
- Visioning 5/1/3
- Transition planning
- 5 min process review

The challenge
For the Leader: *How do I deliver this message?*

For the Community: *How can I get through this without changing?*

Evidence of completion?
Leadership Community trying to maintain the status quo.

Leader thwarted or tricked into believing others are engaged.

Focus questions
Where are we now?
What does the future look like?
What are the first steps?

Sign of progress?
- Leader motivating not just scaring people
- Challenge is explicitly framed
- Ice is broken and trust is growing
- Small groups are working from the past to the future
- Positive behaviour in conversations

Tips

- Don't let people drop in and out of your meeting. It is an organic process. To make sense of it and to build a sense of identity around the group, all of the team members need to be present full time in all the sessions. We have been to far too many meetings where people "pop in", get only part of the picture and end up disrupting the flow of discussions as a result and going away misinformed about where the team are. These people also disrupt the agreed actions at a later date.
- Spend plenty of time as a leader preparing the "framing" session. It is a critical step in getting the team to understand your motivation and intent as a leader. Allow lots of time for question and answer. This gives you a chance to demonstrate exactly what you know and what you don't. People will appreciate your honesty.

Second phase: *Lame response and making the second call …*

Fable Part 4

The Chiefs returned to their villages, but instead of doing what they had agreed, they said to their people: *"Do not worry. Nothing has changed"*. Soon their people began to suffer: the rains were light again, food stocks were running out and doubts grew within them.

When the young 'lion' realised the Chiefs had failed to act he became really angry. Waving his stick once more, he called on the Chiefs a second time: *"You have to accept that things have changed. We need to build a new future together and fast"*. He boldly took charge of the seed supply, sending more to the few chiefs who were adapting to suit the reduced pattern of rain.

At this, the simmering resentment of the hippos erupted. Some wanted to fight him for his high-handedness, others were afraid because he had shown his power, and one or two fell asleep because it was just too frightening.

The Challenge

It's as if you are in a dream with a crowd of starving people and there is a door with a big sign on it saying "FOOD". You point to it but you're invisible. No-one goes there as if they want to continue suffering. You're desperate for a response. Do you shout louder, throw buckets of cold water over people, shine bright lights in their eyes? What will make a difference?

Tony: Our story

Arriving in an utterly unfamiliar and unpredictable place is how I experienced the second phase. Cameroon is one of the poorest countries on earth, and puzzles economists because unlike Botswana, Chile, India and countless other poor countries, it continues to get poorer. It is a nasty shock after the relative comfort and sophistication of Kenya, and on top of this, it is one of the rainiest places on earth. Through my taxi window I watched the baffling array of people on the muddy roadside: a skinny woman carefully roasting one tiny piece of sweet corn for sale, a couple of beaming lads balancing shoes on their heads as an eye-catching advertisement for the trainers in a big bag they dragged behind them, and a woman in a stunning bright purple and white printed wrap-around dress, head erect and wrapped proudly in a matching fabric, tip-toeing between puddles.

Godlove, our taxi driver, demands an extra 12,000 Francs "for gas" on top of our fare. We reluctantly agree. A few hundred metres later police stop the taxi to "fine" him for wrong registration plates, but Godlove expertly escapes their clutches. Repeatedly, the cab lurches alarmingly into fast oncoming traffic to avoid deep puddles, and then pulls up by a stall where Godlove butters up a plump, old machete wielding woman. He moves two big bunches of bananas towards his car, then the woman, objecting to the price Godlove offers, waves her arms screaming: *"Why you want to hurt me?"* at which Godlove, feigning indifference, starts the engine as if to leave. This draws a weary nod of assent from the lady. Godlove pays, loads his bananas and drives off laughing.

Drawing up to our hotel in Douala, Cameroon's second city, it is dark and we see scantily clad girls draped over the bonnets of bright yellow taxis parked on the hotel forecourt. The following morning drawn to my window by voices, I see a gang of men in matching yellow polo shirts and brown shorts jogging and chanting at the same time. I don't know what to make of it. It doesn't look like a sports team training. Could they be prisoners? A work gang off to a shift at the nearby docks? An army unit? I was in the grip of culture shock and honestly I had no idea.

These glimpses tell you that survival isn't easy here and as I try to turn to the work in hand, I'm wondering: how would you really help someone in such circumstances? Is facilitation even useful or do people just need money? If the taxi driver had paid more for the bananas, or if we had bribed the police, what difference would this have made by tomorrow? Wouldn't the police just want more handouts? Something more is needed to change their fortunes – a different way of operating, a new mindset.

Ben and I arrive to find Philip in full action mode: busy, impatient and deeply frustrated. In spite of creating their vision and transition plan for the merger in Nairobi, in the ensuing months, his 30 leaders had done little. Their behaviour seemed irrational because they were in real danger of losing income and having to close, not just a few product lines but whole offices, of having new systems and strategies imposed, of turning away loyal customers and losing capable staff. Why didn't they act to save themselves?

With a few close colleagues, Philip had taken charge of the sensitive question of which "core" products to continue and which "peripheral" products to kill, but he was caught now because he realised he could not force product changes on the countries without turning his 500 staff into victims. Ian was one of this small brave group pushing the change forward:

> *"There were a number of influencers, Philip would have been one. And I was one of a group of people who were pushing the process forward. Putting it simply, with better projects operating in the country, better designed and reaching more people, our impact could be strengthened and our profile raised".*

The reticence of the wider leadership team seemed to invite Philip to impose decisions but he knew this would be self-defeating both for them and ultimately for him. He must wake them up to the new realities if he was to harness their energy, knowledge and experience to deliver effective and sustainable change. He wanted his staff to be leaders working together to transform their situation, but how were we to do this? This was the immediate question before us: how do we get the penny to drop so that 30 people in the leadership community really step up and take on a leadership role for the whole team of 500?

The meeting rooms of the hotel in Douala looked like sheds. There was wildlife from the pool area running through gaps under the doors. I saw a fat bright green lizard and Ben saw a rat. As the meeting assembled, I looked into the faces of 30 leaders and saw with horror how many had changed since Nairobi. I turned to Philip who shrugged and said "that's what we have to deal with". Country Directors tend to take three to four year postings so he had lost a few and would continue to do so throughout this process. On top of this, he had sacked one Country Director for good reasons that he was not free to divulge to the rest of the group. Finally, many of the Country Directors had decided to bring different African senior managers from the last meeting so as to share the privilege of travel and expose more people to the leadership decisions.

Philip, Ben and I had agreed a shared approach to change based on "engagement" which says that if you involve people in creating a collective goal, defining their roles, plans and success measures, then they are more likely to perform because their work is meaningful and fulfilling rather than imposed drudgery. This was at the other end of the spectrum from a "bureaucratic approach" which says that if a plan has been written up and made "official" then magically everyone will know it and work by it! But we needed the core leadership group to understand "engagement" if we were to make it work. Our advice to Philip was, in future, to ask Country Directors to bring the same African senior manager each time so as to stabilise this group.

Philip opened the meeting on an upbeat note, once again framing the challenges facing the region and the need to unlock the power of this group. After Nairobi, we agreed with Philip to work on inculcating the habits of high performance teams and began a teamwork simulation to get people connecting and reflecting on their team behaviours. This addressed Philip's stated aim of using these meetings to build the capacity of the team to collectively respond to the challenges they faced not just in these meetings but in the months between. We described eight behaviours that help top teams perform (see Tools, *Holding Up the Mirror*) and gave out laminated cards for easy reference.

The team enjoyed the simulation but only as an ice-breaker, and overall they performed it badly. It was a struggle to get them to focus on how their behaviour had contributed to their poor performance. They seemed happily distracted from the serious issues they expected to be tackling. Nonetheless, table facilitators appointed from within the leadership team, persisted and succeeded in getting the groups to make a contract to use the behaviours (active listening, questioning, summarising, challenging, supporting etc) that would most quickly bring the real issues into the room.

The mood continued upbeat and in an aside, Ben whispered to me *"They're in denial"*. Yes, the jollity and false confidence exhibited by the team were clear signs that they were avoiding the threat they faced, but a review of progress on the merger brought a less frivolous tone. Although, things were said to be moving fast, the individual country businesses were still not aligned to the regional and corporate priorities. The region was more a concept than a reality. Someone said that the merger was taking away their freedom, another that unless we can demonstrate relevance we will lose key sources of income, and yet another, that trust is an issue across this team.

Then a great wave of excitement rippled round the room when we heard that London had won the 2012 Olympic bid. We continued the work and by the time we closed the first day the overall impression was of people starting to get past being polite and beginning to raise issues. That evening Philip reflected that the day's discussions had been "difficult" with unpleasantness from one or two people, one table had low energy, on another people were taking turns but holding back, and on another a few noisy people were dominating, leaving the others quiet.

The second day started with the shocking news of bombs in London. Immediately this became a focus. We had to break for people to check on London-based friends and relatives, but on finding most of the phone lines jammed, we resumed in some uncertainty. As previously in Nairobi, we would find that the mood could turn suddenly and unpredictably nasty.

We brought in a group of external customers: young business people from the "outside world" who we thought could have a waking-up effect on the group, but there was little obvious impact. Then a head office visitor, struggling with our ground rule of "no PowerPoint", delivered the news that there was a massive restructuring underway in the UK and that HQ would begin to work radically differently. The immediate lack of response to one of the biggest head office changes in living memory seemed eerie but slowly, as we invited reactions, furrowed brows turned into angry questions that seemed to rail against the new era dawning:

"This is not the job I joined up to do. Are we just going to be reduced to administrators?"

"Why are you pushing us – is the fast pace really necessary?"

"Are you really asking us to discuss this or have you made all the decisions already?"

"Is this the right way to go?"

The anger showed it was becoming harder for people to believe they could continue the status quo but they were still holding tightly onto freedoms they had enjoyed for decades and onto a tacit understanding amongst them that someone, somewhere should continue to fund their diverse activities.

The big and difficult message was: *"you will cease to exist if you do not deliver results"* and this was bringing people back to uncomfortable questions such as: *What are we really here for? And, how do we get enough income to really make a difference?* Although the large questions of purpose and impact had already been answered by head office in a five year strategy paper (*"cultural relations reaching millions more people"*) this had not brought clarity to the minds of these 30 people or the 500 country-based staff who each had a different way of describing what the company does. In this region, 500 staff were busy doing hundreds of commissioned projects and they were angry to be told their work did not produce the needed impact. The threat that their projects would be stopped made them indignant, hurt or insecure. Looking back, Akello from West Africa said she felt angry and she was asking herself:

"What's wrong with what we are doing already? Isn't it enough, isn't it appreciated?"

Gail, a country director from Ethiopia, felt similarly:

"The anxiety was that there'd been all this stuff going on that was perfectly successful and why suddenly do we have to do something different".

Historically, 11 Country Offices with a public service mission, facing more than their fair share of the world's worst problems (poverty, conflict, insecurity, disease, lack of skills, lack of democracy, justice, corruption) had a queue of people knocking on their doors with worthy projects. Much of this work had been funded by the UK taxpayer. However today, over two thirds of the organisation's funding is from new sources: fee-paying customers, partners such as the European Union and the World Bank, and from a wide array of corporate clients including many multinational organisations. But this pulls the teams in new directions, not necessarily towards the strategy. People deeply committed to their work were contemplating, grappling, trying to make sense of the change, weighing up options and understandably finding it uncomfortable to let go. There was still a huge amount of anxiety in the group. As Binte from Senegal said:

"I had the fear of a cut in our budget and more being given to bigger countries so that the amounts allocated for my country would be small … That's where the anxiety was. Initially, there were fears of maybe a reduction in the staff, of job losses, also of lack of capacity to deliver some of the products. Some staff felt 'oh this is like removing me from my own country setting and exposing me to a wider context… do I have the skills to fit the challenge?'"

Ben and I took the loss of good humour, tunnel vision and anger as signs of an old paradigm shaking and breaking apart, but for Philip the arrows pierced deeply. Outside during the break he whispered earnestly to me about how members of the group were irritating him with their "feed me" attitudes. It seemed he was getting caught in his own trap. He had been challenging people to speak out and now they were responding honestly but he didn't like the negativity of their messages. He noticed "elephants in the room" including some fear and suspicion that arose from the sacking of a Country Director but his not being allowed to announce why. We could see how one person had been speaking up in protest for another whose local office was closing. As people began to speak out, the exchanges had become increasingly unpleasant but some people were still "hiding under the blanket".

Philip's frustration came across to me as irrational and a further sign of the shockwaves that ripple through everyone in a group, including the leader, when a significant mental block is shifting. I reminded him that earlier we had seen people polite, avoiding issues, distracted into digressions and departures and lifted by denial into false jollity and that the anger coming up from the group was a positive sign of people starting to actively engage. I reassured him that the messages from customers and the UK underlined the legitimacy of changes he was leading. In other words, his team did not just see their Regional Director going mad but that actually, he was lined up with the UK and pushing things in a direction they needed to go.

After the break, Philip pushed back with firmness bordering on anger, by confirming that future funding, instead of coming from the UK, would flow through his office, and that countries needed to get used to new levels of accountability, with targets signed up to actually being met. Some uncomfortable facts about funding were put on the table: *"over 50% disappears into supporting the infrastructure, leaving 50% that is frittered away"* on delivering countless small local products which are *"largely invisible and without measured or obvious impact"*.

Unbelievably, I noticed someone asleep at the back of the room! Instead of leaders we still had a room full of victims: some complacent, other confused, shocked or overwhelmed, some completely shutting down and others exploding angrily as they found it increasingly difficult to remain in denial. The eight value-creating behaviours we had shown people the previous morning had been temporarily put to one side and people were disconnecting, sulking or snarling at each other. Now the wave of emotion was affecting me too. Unusually, I was simmering with anger, finding it hard to focus and I could see that Ben was apoplectic!

Our dinner outing that evening was also a bit of a disaster. We climbed onto a private bus in time to reach a local riverside restaurant where at sunset you see the beautiful peak of Mount Cameroon reflected in the water. Somehow the driver misunderstood, got us lost and we missed the sunset.

When we arrived at the restaurant it was shut and they had no record of our booking. Finally, we persuaded the restaurant to open but it still took over an hour for food to come.

The third and final day we pushed the victims to shape up. I held up the mirror contrasting their behaviour the previous day with that of high performing teams. They struggled. One person complained of "jumps in the programme" asking how today's work related to the previous day's discussions. During a report back from a sub-group, two people fell into an argument while others stood back and let them.

On a positive note, we were succeeding in getting more minority voices in the room, but usually in dissent. Philip, Ben and I found we could rely on the table facilitators to make constructive contributions and we did see a few other brave people step forward making quite impressive presentations but being denied the encouragement they deserved from colleagues. After we had painstakingly listed by name hundreds of existing products covering all the customer-facing activities of all eleven country operations, clustered and sorted them into "core" (high impact, central to the mission of the organisation – to continue) and "peripheral" (low impact, tangential to the mission of the organisation – to be stopped), we gained agreement on the few big cross-regional products to take forward.

This left team members with some new dilemmas, asking *"Do I want to be part of this? Is this what I joined this organisation to do? What is left of my role? Do I have a say or have all the decisions been taken?"*. They resented being asked to kill off hundreds of products they loved. For some however, this was a turning point. As Akello said:

> *"I actually had a thought of moving on to do something else but then at the same time I felt one voice in me was telling me 'no this is a new challenge, if you have the chance to do it, face this new challenge and it will probably teach me to do things differently'".*

Ian from West Africa, who had been more deeply involved in the work leading up to Douala, was more upbeat about the meeting:

> *"People did begin to see the benefits. In those months prior to this meeting, a number of barriers were broken, personal relationships were developing and people were beginning to see action taking place. Obviously people have commitment to doing things and don't like the idea of stopping doing them but there was general recognition we were not getting far with our local products".*

Most agreed that our three days together had been a long slog as we proved beyond doubt that an era was passing. Gabriel later observed the moment when change hits you emotionally:

"It was a real shock for me. After people understood the reasons for the change intellectually, it was only later that they really got what it meant for them personally and it was like a mini-explosion!"

Old ways of working were no longer possible, and people were not happy about it. At the end of the meeting there was a sad and defeated tone to people's closing comments. The "leaders" somehow felt abandoned. Philip acknowledged he was asking a lot, recognised how difficult the meeting had been for everyone and signalled that the teamwork they had started needed to be continued at a distance after everyone went home.

Ben and I went home cross but not surprised that the new people who had not had the benefit of Nairobi had failed to "get it". An ambitious programme, combined with unexpected events, had put the group into overload and they had reacted first by reaching for their phones, then dipping in and out and finally by appearing sad and confused, sensing trouble ahead. In spite of packing too much in, the end of workshop feedback was not bad, but we were not able to feel proud or professionally fulfilled by the outcome. We could not be confident that County Directors would help their staff reprioritise heavy workloads in order to make space for the new regional tasks.

■ How do you approach this phase?

We tried to understand why this group had created and signed up to a "transition plan" in Nairobi but done little or nothing since. It seemed that, as in the fable, the Chiefs had gone back home and told their people not to worry. As a result, nothing much was happening. Life in "the outlying villages" was continuing as usual.

Changing attitudes and behaviour

"A leopard can't change its spots" is said with disappointment or bitter cynicism when a person, whether an alcoholic, a gambler, a dieter or an unfaithful partner lets us down by failing to change in the way that they promised and we hoped. We were disappointed but not yet in despair at the inaction since Nairobi, partly because of the wealth of evidence that proves change is possible.

For example Kurt Lewin, a pioneer in social psychology who escaped from Nazi Germany, demonstrated that for a group to perform intelligently it needs a particular kind of leader who is democratic not autocratic, and to bring about change the leader needs to "unfreeze" the group bringing an emotional stir-up to "break open the shell of complacency and self-righteousness". Lewin also noted that the group a person belongs to is the "ground" for their perceptions, feelings and actions; and the sum total of all the motivations, conflicts and forces in a group he called the "group field". So our job was to involve people, stir them up, and in the end to transform the "group field" so that each person invests their own energy in making the merger a success (Lewin, 1997).

Leon Festinger, a social psychologist followed Lewin with a theory of Cognitive Dissonance, in which he proposed that people experience psychological pain when their behaviour does not match their attitudes (Festinger, 1957). For example, if a person believes that smoking is bad for them (their "attitude") yet they continue smoking (their "behaviour") then this creates a pressure which is likely to result either in a change to their attitude ("smoking is not bad for everyone") or in their behaviour (giving up smoking). If participants in our meeting wrongly believed the work they had been doing in their countries was achieving the needed impact, Philip the leader could address either their attitudes or their behaviour to bring about change. For example, he could address attitudes by presenting evidence that the work was not having the intended impact. At the same time, he could address behaviour by getting people to try out something more effective like helping one another in bigger cross-regional project teams. Currently, people had neither the relevant information to challenge their attitude nor direct experience of alternative ways of working to challenge their behaviour.

Letting go of the past

Since birth we have all been experiencing change in one form or another and it continues to our graves. We learn to change through participating in rites of passage such as 21st and 40th birthdays, moving homes and jobs, weddings and funerals. But why is change sometimes so painful? John Bowlby (1951) describes how small children attach themselves to their carer, almost as ducks imprint on whoever is present at a critical moment. Later without realising, we become attached to our home, workplace, friends, workmates, even to our habits and ways of being in control. During change we must let go of the people and things we value, and this entails our identities and boundaries being fundamentally re-arranged. We find ourselves painfully betwixt and between, being "lost" before being "found". So how can we help ourselves and others to re-align and find themselves more quickly?

The early part of a merger or change programme is often difficult and slow, in part because leaders, impatient for new beginnings, fail to honour the amount of time and support their staff need to make sense of what is happening, to let go of the past and to move on. William Bridges (1980) building on earlier work by Elizabeth Kubler-Ross (1973) into bereavement, explained the difference between "change" which happens in the outer world and "transition" which happens inside the skin and takes a little longer:

> *"(Leaders of change)... often forget that while the first task of Change Management is to understand the destination and how to get there, the first task of Transition Management is to convince people to leave home. You'll save yourself a lot of grief if you remember that"* (Bridges, 1980).

Bridges describes three phases in transition management: letting go, a neutral zone, and then, new beginnings. "Letting go" is the first priority and in doing so, the leader needs to clarify what is ending. In psychological terms, it is the opposite of a merger. It is a "clean separation" which requires a shared clarity of what is finishing and what isn't. It entails a celebration of success, an acknowledgement of the contribution from those in the team, and the leaving behind of emotional baggage such as blame, guilt or sorrow.

Looking back with hindsight, we did not address "letting go" directly enough in Nairobi. Letting go is emotional and it is natural for people to be defensive, perhaps in fight, flight or freeze, giving strong reactions. By the end of a Douala workshop that was deeply frustrating, most were grumpily realising the inevitable but still isolated in grief for what they were losing.

Reading the signs of resistance

Without strong direction from us, the group would use up the entire meeting time talking without reaching any decisions. At the same time, Philip kept trying to push the group into action. We had been dragging the group to produce the transition plan while missing some of the signs of resistance from the group and in approaching the decisions to "decommission" some of the existing products, we noticed the team were fearfully holding onto the status quo.

What were the subtle and "easy to miss" signs of resistance? William Schutz, a psychologist who helped the US Navy overcome problems of conflict in submarine crews, identifies the following signs of resistance: holding rigidly to my position, not listening, misinterpreting, withholding, feeling misunderstood, being easily irritated or angered, avoiding certain topics, not wanting to probe, becoming confused, losing my sense of humour (Schutz, 1994). He noticed that each of us has different defence mechanisms and identified six defensive postures people tend to take:

- Denier – "there are no problems"
- Victim – "I am offended because other people are behaving aggressively/ unreasonably"
- Critic – "I know better than you and I pick up on everything that is not perfect e.g. your grammar, your stupid remark or your weak idea"
- Self-blamer – "everything that happens is my fault"
- Helper – "I look for anyone else that needs help whether they want it or not"
- Demander – "reassure me that I'm OK and there's nothing wrong with me"

A psychologically healthy adult response to a changing environment is to be curious, self-aware and discriminating – a person assimilates the information and resources that meet their true need. A leader has to extend an individual's awareness of their need, and support them in making choices.

Working through resistance

When resistance is identified then how do you best address it? Arnold Mindell's method is to recognise that each individual experiencing resistance needs to move through three different positions ("as self", "as other" and "as fly on the wall") before they can resolve their inner conflict (Mindell, 1992). A facilitator's job is to help a person to express these positions through a process of reflecting on these questions:

- What is your point of view?
- What is your colleague's point of view?
- What do we each need now?

During this process people often make illogical and contradictory statements and can get quite emotional but the process itself allows a psychological shift to take place. Typically, not only does a person feel better afterwards but they are then ready and motivated to take up their responsibility as a leader. Reflecting back on what she had learnt from the process we went through, Foluke, one of the African senior managers summarises the approach we took like this:

> *"I was resolved not to be deterred by resistance and not to ignore it either. But to understand it and so do something about it".*

Creating a sense of urgency

John Kotter a Harvard professor who studied 100 organisations (most of which failed in their efforts to transform), defines the first step of transformation as "creating a sense of urgency" which convinces at least 75% of the leadership community of the need for change (Kotter, 2002). Typically, leaders are reluctant to give the negative information people need to persuade them change is necessary. He went on to describe eight steps that need to be completed before an organisation has completed a transformation:

1. Creating a sense of urgency → we must do something
2. Build the guiding team → the right people on board to drive the change
3. Get the vision right → give the guiding team a compelling vision to direct the effort
4. Communicate for buy-in → sending credible messages and walking the talk
5. Empower action → removing barriers to people behaving differently
6. Create short-term wins → fast results to diffuse cynicism
7. Don't let up → not allowing urgency to sag, creating wave after wave of change
8. Make change stick → reshaping culture, practices, norms and values.

▓ What are the signs of progress in this phase?

1. When team members are exposed to new points of view (as in customer research) and experiment with new behaviours (as in using new behaviour in teams to bring the real issues out onto the table) (Festinger).

2. When team members are "bitching and moaning", expressing a mixed up range of mostly negative emotions both about the past and the future, showing they are beginning to detach and re-evaluate the past. Later, when this mood has passed they may be ready to celebrate the ending, clearly identifying what is over, and what they are bringing from the past with them into the future (Bridges).
3. When the subtle signs of resistance are identified and people are challenged to get in touch with their true needs (Schutz).
4. When in spite of the corporate urgency, team members are given enough time, challenge and support to fully contemplate and explore their dilemmas around what is changing, the benefits and costs of changing and not changing, finding the real options and choices they have, leading them into a state of mind where they are prepared to change (Mindell).
5. When at least 75% of the leadership population are genuinely convinced that change is necessary (Kotter).

■ What tools can you use?

In this second phase, the four tools which follow give the leader ways to engage others in addressing these key questions: *What new realities do we need to wake up to? How do we get back in control? What can we keep? What do we need to let go of and how?*

No 1: Direct contact with stakeholders requiring change

People need to know what is changing and to understand why. Rather than simply delivering second-hand wake-up calls through Philip, or through head office emails, we decided to bring specific people (customers from a new target group, and a sponsor from head office) into the room to deliver "the need for change" message directly. This allowed Philip as leader to adopt a less adversarial and more facilitative position, helping participants grapple with the contradictions and making meaning out of it.

No 2: Three circles

When participants are struggling with change and they feel like victims we ask them in side conversations, what is in their three circles (Marlier and Parker, 2008):

1. The "outer circle" which is sometimes called "circle of doom" because it is the negative stuff that they cannot influence (see Covey, 1989, pp. 81–88). We offer them five minutes to "bitch and moan" about what is there, but then suggest they stop worrying and let go of concerns they can do nothing about.
2. We then ask them what is in their inner "circle of control", pointing out that for most people, even the richest and most powerful on earth, there are few things that they totally control without receiving permission from, or putting out their influence towards, others.
3. We ask them how they can extend their middle "circle of influence". Who do you need to connect with and influence and on which topics?

Typically people report feeling better and more proactive after this exercise.

No 3: Holding up the mirror

For any team going through change, open, exploratory conversations are necessary. In the denial phase, as they face the harsh facts, buried issues and emotions need to be raised to the surface. In a team, this means each person needs to listen, question and connect more effectively just when their defences are causing them to fight, flee or freeze. To achieve this, we show people how to see and speak about behaviour. This gives them a greater sense of control even when they are experiencing some quite strong emotions in the "letting go" phase. So we conduct a short business simulation in which performance depends on information-sharing and teamworking and we teach people how to use eight value-building behaviours (active listening, open questions, summarising, support, challenge, clarifying, timeout and review) that give an edge to high performance teams. We appoint and carefully brief Table Facilitators to "work" the value-building behaviours, reinforcing them through a behavioural contract and behavioural reviews. In each review, the facilitator "holds up the mirror" to show a group how they can adjust their behaviour to raise their performance.

No 4: Managing endings – Timeline

When a group is holding onto the past they become stuck, stressed, depressed, numb or low in energy. You can use a tool called Timeline as follows:

1. Each person identifies their key events (good and bad) since joining the organisation, writes them each on a separate post-it and posts them on a chronological line on a long wall-chart.
2. The group gathers round, asks questions, looks for themes.
3. Each person then shares their proudest and sorriest moments, and also declares something they needed to leave behind (a behaviour or an attitude) and something they want to bring with them (a memento, a skill or a quality) into the future. As they take turns to make these declarations, they physically step over a line into the future.

■ What is the evidence of completing this phase?

- Ideally, all members of a team will have identified what to leave behind and what to bring with them. They will have drawn a line that marks the decision to change and stepped over the line from the past into the future.
- The leadership community may still feel sad, defeated, fragmented and lost. It's an ending with a deep sense of loss and this opens the possibility of a proactive phase to come
- Realistically the leader and facilitators may be angry, having received the group's resistance.

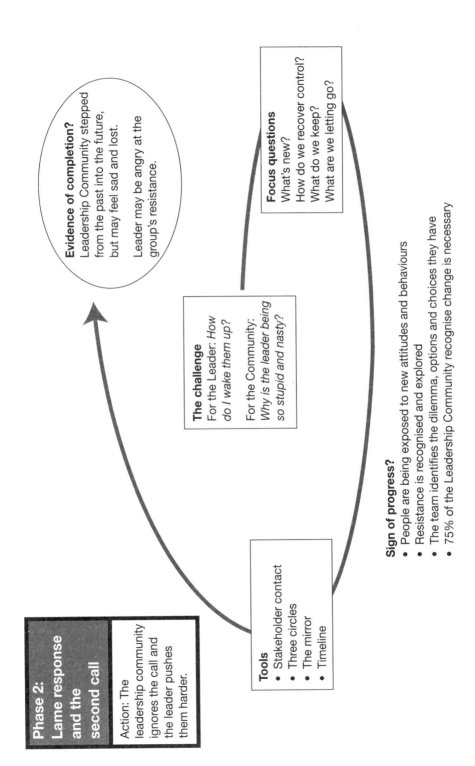

Evidence of completion?
Leadership Community stepped from the past into the future, but may feel sad and lost.

Leader may be angry at the group's resistance.

Focus questions
What's new?
How do we recover control?
What do we keep?
What are we letting go?

The challenge
For the Leader: *How do I wake them up?*

For the Community:
Why is the leader being so stupid and nasty?

Sign of progress?
• People are being exposed to new attitudes and behaviours
• Resistance is recognised and explored
• The team identifies the dilemma, options and choices they have
• 75% of the Leadership Community recognise change is necessary

Tools
• Stakeholder contact
• Three circles
• The mirror
• Timeline

**Phase 2:
Lame response
and the
second call**

Action: The leadership community ignores the call and the leader pushes them harder.

Tips

- Strike a balance between focusing on internal change and external delivery, and keep pushing for action.
- Don't worry when people express strong negative feelings – it can often mean they are moving their attitudes and coming on board.
- Seek facilitator/coach support to work through the negative emotion coming in your direction from others during the denial phase.

5

Third phase: *The leadership community falls apart ... then steps up ...*

The Fable Part 5

For months the hippos remained angry, some were confused, then the mood turned to defeat as they felt the passing of a happy era. Starved of information, their people both in the East and the West felt more and more anxious.

Then happily one day the young chief discovered "a thing of beauty" – a new seed needing less rain, and despite his frustration, he gathered the Chiefs a third time.

Remembering an old saying from his tribe, "One head does not contain all the wisdom", he decided there and then to change his approach. Instead of waving his stick, he simply pointed to the declining food stores and calmly stated: *"There is no going back: unless we accept this, we will all die"*. He asked the Chiefs to sit together as their fathers and mothers had done in the old days, East alongside West, to decide on a solution.

They were gloomy but as the Chiefs grappled with the challenge a new mood took hold and they declared: *"We have had a change of heart. We are all in the same boat and we need to work together!"*.

The Challenge

It seems that all we have achieved so far is to make people unhappy, confused, scattered in all directions. How do we bring them together again and support them in becoming strong, confident individuals who, as part of a team, know how to change their fortunes?

Tony: Our story

During the months following their cold shower in Douala, more of the leaders sensed the new opportunity in the air including Gail from Ethiopia:

"People started challenging each other on why we were continuing to do some of the stuff that we'd been doing for years just because we'd always been doing it".

Already old certainties were breaking down and a new fluidity was being created in people's sense of who and what they were. Key individuals within the team – enthused through direct conversations and contact with Philip – were buying in to the change. As Gabriel from Senegal says:

"Philip is results focused, and is very energetic, supportive and consistent in that support. His attitude is contagious – I caught that bug and went on to infuse the rest of the team".

There was more clarity amongst the team on the direction they were taking and the impact of not changing. Otim from Kenya noticed that Philip's leadership message, so often repeated, was slowly sinking in to work its magic:

"Personally, when you're moving me from one place to another, I need to understand why you're moving me so that I can help in the movement. So, to me that clarity in the message was the key".

If progress seemed slow it was not just that the leaders were being stubborn. The team was constantly changing as people were moving on to new posts elsewhere; their replacements arriving needed to figure out what to do and why. When Mark joined the region as a Country Director, he was confronted with a clear challenge:

"When I arrived here my line manager told me this was the worst performing country in the region with people having worked here a long time becoming protective and silo-ed. So the first thing I had to do was restructure. It meant losing about half the people we had. You do have to change the people – not all of them – to let go those who don't want to be part of it and nurture those who do".

Looking at the poor performance in the wider region, Mark was sceptical about whether and how it could be addressed:

"Politically this region was a fairly low priority and had tiny amounts of money available. To put it bluntly, we were in bad shape, rudderless and a bit self-indulgent and there were only two ways to go: further down, or up. My thought about the change was 'here we go again' because we'd been shuffling this stuff around like packs of cards for the last decade".

Each member of the leadership team clearly needed a firm grasp of the issues, the strength of a supportive band of colleagues around them and to understand what their individual contribution should be on the journey the entire team was being asked to take.

In the wake of Tony Blair's Commission for Africa and the Gleneagles Summit, the East and West Africa operation had secured new funding from head office to develop some big, new products. This was good news but it had the knock-on effect of complicating the annual budgeting exercise. Philip needed countries to understand the new arrangements and for country directors to sign-up to the business they needed to deliver over the next five years.

By now, we were used to the group of 30 leaders talking endlessly and failing to reach agreement. So, with the team's next meeting in Addis Ababa fast approaching, we scheduled a full day at the start to thrash out how each country would contribute to delivering the regional targets. Determined not to run out of time, we were prepared to spend the whole three day meeting on this single issue if necessary.

Before the meeting, we asked ourselves how far we were in turning the 30 leaders into a team. They had left Douala with their heads down, apparently defeated and fragmented as if the former, superficial bonds that had held them together had been broken without any new bonds yet in place. In spite of this, Philip was getting a positive message from head office that the merger in his region appeared to be going well. This wasn't happening by chance. Like any good chief, Philip was very aware that he had to keep a firm eye on what was happening in the world outside the "villages" in his region. He knew that if the change programme was to work he had to quickly demonstrate benefits to customers and business improvements to his bosses.

Working closely with a small group of change enthusiasts from both East and West, and with people in headquarters, Philip had started the process of designing the new product range. Given that he was from "the East", he had made special efforts with the "West" to ensure his people there felt the benefits of being part of this group and supported in their roles. For Ian, a country director from West Africa, this was already a big improvement on the old arrangements:

"I felt enormous relief actually…in various ways. Although it is far removed from the days of steam liner and the telegraph, those country director jobs are quite isolating. Having more communication and more support available I think was a genuine benefit".

Those in small operations had been afraid of being swallowed up by a big, new region where they would simply disappear off the radar. To counter this, Philip made sure these countries had his attention, as Binte from Senegal describes:

"It was natural to have that kind of fear, especially if your country is small. Philip understood and, funnily enough, it turned out to be the opposite".

So, yes, there was progress. But, we had evidence that despite our efforts so far, this was not yet a team. People were still not spontaneously linking, pooling resources or creating solutions to common problems. There was something more required if we were to achieve a deeper level of buy-in and create a level of regional teamworking that could drive the organisation forward and be sustained over time.

A couple of days before the Addis Ababa meeting, riots were reported following the disputed Ethiopian election result. This was followed by the arrest of thousands of students, teachers and opposition political leaders. Uncertainty existed about whether the meeting could go ahead. Up until the last minute, we were advised to check the Foreign Office website before getting on the plane but in the event, there was nothing to stop us travelling.

We arrived in a grand marble palace of a hotel set far back from the street. The thin air of high altitude Addis Ababa meant that climbing stairs left you embarrassingly out of breath. A day trip out to the Blue Nile Gorge gave us a glimpse of the rural Ethiopian Highlands. Our expectations were turned upside down when we saw field after pretty field of harvested grain neatly stacked and ready to be brought to market. In contrast, Addis was more difficult on the eye: donkey carts on the streets, exhausted women carrying small bundles of sticks for firewood having walked many kilometres simply to earn a few coins. From a distance, we saw armed troops racing to break up a riot, abandoned buses and uniformed pupils locked out of a school. Like Douala, it struck us once again, that this was the business environment in which these teams in the organisation were doing their work day after day, week after week.

Somehow, the trip out made what we had to do inside the conference room seem a little easier and underlined the real worth of the work we were doing to build the strength of this group. While Ben and I were at the Blue Nile Gorge, Philip spent the day rushing from one pre-meeting to another. Since Douala, Philip had created the Regional Steering Group – a small group of senior managers taken from within the Regional Leadership Team – whose role was to oversee progress on the merger and change programme and to give advice to Philip on the way forward. We had agreed to have a pre-meeting with Philip and this group as part of the preparation for the workshop.

When we caught up with Philip for a few minutes before sitting down with the Steering Group he seemed quite wound up and distracted. He was dissatisfied because in spite of the progress made in terms of business results, the group of 30 still did not feel to him like a real team. For the last twelve months, we had been dragging and pushing them: now we needed them to unleash their energy, realising the benefits of working together.

Given this ambition the Steering Group meeting did not get off to the most promising start. One member began an animated argument with Philip saying: "*It's all about trust. That is part of your role Philip not to frighten people about possible job losses. You can feel their resistance building*". Nevertheless, Philip was uncompromising about sticking to corporate targets for impacting more customers and becoming more cost-effective. To his by now sullen and switched off colleague, Philip re-emphasised the fact that the targets were given and the team needed to work together to make choices about how to deliver them.

Ben and I pressed on to brief Steering Group members to stay out of adversarial squabbles in the three day meeting with the group of 30 and instead we asked them to build on the special role they had started to play as coaches in Douala: alert to any defensive behaviour, listening, questioning and summarising to bring real issues to the surface. We expected from what had just happened that some would find this difficult.

What I did not realise until later was that, in the run up to the meeting, Philip had been reflecting hard on his role and impact on the group. During this time, he had a significant insight – "one head does not contain all the wisdom" – that meant he wanted to make a shift in his leadership style. He no longer needed to push the regional agenda so hard as he could now channel regional funds to where they would have the most impact. His Finance Director had prepared a single page financial spreadsheet (jokingly called "the thing of beauty") for each of the 11 countries, and which when added up, gave the total budget for the region for the next five years. Instead of holding this close and trying to push and command the change, Philip had decided to open the books and offer it to everyone, then to coach (instead of 'tell') his people on how to use this information to move the business forward. This shift in Philip's approach made a huge difference to what followed.

As the group of 30 assembled the following morning, they seemed ready to get down to business and by lunchtime were quite upbeat, but the afternoon proved more difficult as participants challenged one another to get creative about how to achieve tough new targets for raising new income and reducing costs. Philip and his immediate staff instead of pushing people became a "coaching resource" called on to clarify "the thing of beauty". Effective though this was, by mid-afternoon, energy levels were dropping as people were getting worried about whether they could reach the targets and unsure about whether they had the capacity to deliver the new products.

By this time, we didn't think the group would be capable of producing much from the day, but the closing plenary at the end of the afternoon surpassed our expectations. Feedback from the team showed that not only had the "thing of beauty" been understood but it was also accepted and liked! While the afternoon had been difficult, the penny had finally dropped that the region had only a finite amount of income available at this point. Most now understood they needed to organise their resources in a much "smarter" way and in collective agreement in order to deliver the required result. They had made a big step towards taking shared accountability for results and action. One of the Country Directors summarised the change of heart that the team had experienced:

"We've realised this afternoon that we are all in the same boat!"

It was a magical moment, as if the group's identity suddenly changed before our very eyes: they were no longer the territorial hippos we had become used to!

In spite of some unanswered questions, this was a major result, both in terms of a strategic agreement to budgeting but also in terms of team personality and strength. That evening the Regional Steering Group worked very effectively in reviewing the day and taking decisions on certain outstanding questions which were announced the following morning. Philip was disappointed that the wider plenary of 30 had been unable to take these decisions, but he acknowledged that he had been unrealistic and with the Steering Group providing a bridge between him and the group of 30, everyone seemed finally to be getting into their stride.

The following day, we gathered round and began by reviewing progress towards regional working and we received an interesting comment from the group:

"This should have been done at the beginning of a meeting because each time there is a little bit of progress to celebrate and we all need to recognise the special contributions that some people are making to this".

At first, hearing a criticism of the programme my reflex was to be defensive and justify the sequence of the workshop but hearing the "we" in the statement and the desire for recognition of a shared venture from the group was very encouraging, and reinforced our sense of an emerging team mentality.

For the next two days, we continued to work on developing the regional products interspersed with some physical "social mapping" activities designed to provoke people in the group of 30 into forging links with colleagues in other countries.

During a break, one of the African senior managers, reflected back to us that part of the group enjoy sitting down discussing while another part *"enjoyed being out of their seats, moving, being expressive"*. As facilitators, we had already catered for these preferences with a good mix of activity and talking in the programme. Looking back, however, we noticed the older more set-in-their-ways Country Directors, were more comfortable expressing themselves in the rough and tumble of strategic, roundtable discussions but awkward in activity that was at all expressive or playful. They wanted to get on with the "real work" of discussion while others were freed up by breaking out into different modes of interaction.

The inability to shift styles seemed not only to betray a lack of understanding of their "real work" as a leadership team, but also to relate to an entrenched hierarchy. Back at home we imagined the old fashioned Country Director "telling" but terribly nicely, filling the air with clever speech, while unwittingly or presumptively stopping a colleague from speaking their mind, yet achieving this pleasantly enough to hold an "inclusive" illusion in place.

When towards the end of the meeting, Wambui, a senior manager from East Africa, took Philip aside and said:

"It's good that the African senior managers are here but you do realise that many of us still don't feel able to fully participate in this meeting and this needs to be addressed if this team is really to work".

... this seemed to make inescapable the contrast between the easy rhetoric about "being inclusive" and a "not-to-be-referred-to" hierarchy of contribution: if you were a woman, African or lower in grade you generally spoke less. As feedback, it felt painfully true, and there was a realisation that in spite of all our efforts as facilitators some issues were still not on the table.

Nevertheless, the meeting ended on a high. Instead of a typical close for the workshop – pulling together a joint action plan – we decided to ask pairs from each country to share "a single action they had passion to implement" on their return. As we went round the room, the energy seemed to build from one person to the next like a series of firecrackers. People were bursting to speak and confidently declaring quite radical things they intended to go back and do. One director declared that "*it was time to clear the decks and get started on the new agenda*". Another committed to complete a difficult reorganisation before the next meeting. Philip had prepared closing words but put them aside. He was delighted and did not want to add anything. It was as if the whole group was smiling.

People gathered around Ben and me at the end expressing their appreciation for a great meeting and conveying their recognition that something special had happened over the last three days. They were now part of something exciting and new – a leadership team – and this was something that they could draw strength from when they went back into their country operations with difficult actions to take.

By the end of the Addis meeting, the team had decided to operate as a region, balance the books and to support one another, while holding countries accountable for their performance. This was undeniable progress. Mark, the sceptical new arrival at Addis, had revised his opinion:

"The advent of the concept of a region suddenly made a huge amount of sense in terms of economies of scale, cooperating in a kind of multilateral sense rather than working country by country where our programmes were very small. Previously, there was no coherence to any of it. It didn't add up to a story".

Yahya from Ghana, who had painstakingly explained to us the importance of pecking order and strong hierarchical leadership in Africa had now experienced the benefits of working as a team:

"You have to create an environment where you have people expressing an idea, moving away from the position of thinking 'I don't want to do anything wrong' to being creative and utilising the resources that we have. You need a leader who gives you the political support to push an idea through, for setting targets and sticking to them. There is an old saying that 'one tree does not make a forest'. The leader has to be quite good at carrying everybody along".

The facilitator-leader collaboration between Philip and me had taken a big step forward during the Addis meeting. We were finding how to work more effectively together. Afterwards I asked him about this and he replied:

"As a leader who is willing to take risks, I tend to see an opportunity or a space and then push fast towards it, but the people I need with me will often close up or block. What the facilitator does then is to embrace the others who are switching off wherever they are and as the facilitator inquires, they soften and the space opens up differently so that you as the leader are not on your own anymore. They are there with you".

I have noticed that ideas come up fast for Philip, he races towards them and sometimes he leaves others behind. While he is operating like this, they cannot step up but in Addis the shift he made, stepping back and listening more meant that people became more engaged, as if responding to his trust in them.

Nevertheless, in spite of the breakthroughs we had made, the comment from Wambui about senior management participation, still hung ominously in the air. Yes, we could make a strong argument that we had become more inclusive but was it good enough? What made it more worrying for me was a sense I got of a refusal to speak about how the targets and decisions agreed at our meeting would actually be communicated and implemented back in countries.

Ben and I went home uplifted by the energy in the closing session and pleased at the progress we had made but I was troubled by the fact that one year after our first meeting in Nairobi there were still "elephants in the room". I wondered if I had been too caught up in the mechanics of facilitating. Did I need to spend more time speaking with individuals to find out the stories and struggles they had been unable to express in public? Yes, the sun had come out after the Douala rain but somehow I still felt that if I looked over my shoulder, storm clouds were hanging worryingly on the horizon.

■ How do you approach this phase?

We needed to bring people together after the disturbing effect of Douala. Linking back to the fable, Philip, like the young chief, was realising he needed to take a different path. He knew that he wanted to galvanise the group so that they could achieve "real teamwork" and make a difference. He realised that continuing to push and provoke was not going to deliver this but it was unclear to him at first exactly what sort of shift he needed to make.

Moving on

Having said goodbye to the past, how do you align your team towards a common goal for the future? Janice Prochaska (Prochaska, 2001) describes a five-stage approach to align attitudes and behaviour in individuals. She calls these Pre-contemplation, Contemplation, Preparation, Action and Maintenance

Initially, a leader like Philip is "ready to get on with it" (in "Action") bringing a change to someone who "has not thought about it yet" (in "Pre-contemplation") and the yawn they receive is not the reaction they hoped for. The temptation is to get angry, frustrated and to push harder for the breakthrough. This is where the leader has to fight their instincts. Instead of pushing, the leader needs to set aside time for the team to work on weighing the options and making their own mind up.

The next job of the leader is to explore realistically with the team both or many sides of a question and work through their defensive reflexes (freeze, fight, flight) which stop them addressing the question. This is called "Contemplation" and here the leader can push, both challenging and supporting the person's exploration and they can expect strong emotional reactions, as at times a person may feel unloved, rejected, angry, hurt, threatened and vulnerable. The leader should not be disappointed if, at this stage, the person fails to behave rationally or proactively. This is normal! Each person is torn apart by opposing instincts: to pull away suspiciously in fear, or to advance trustfully or excitedly and embrace the new.

In many mergers, the discomfort of Contemplation is prolonged until the moment when a new layer of jobs is announced. When a person recognises the "Choice Point" (e.g. choosing whether to apply, whether to accept a job offered, whether to take a package or a new direction) then they move from being "lost" to "found", and their new identity emerges bringing joy, relief and a new sense of excitement. By the end of "Contemplation", the penny has dropped and a person is ready to move into making plans for what's next ("Preparation").

Preparing for action

Having been through the "Pre-contemplation" and "Contemplation" phases of Prochaska's model in Nairobi and Douala, most participants arrived in Addis with the penny having dropped, recognising that the merger had happened and that regionalisation was underway. In Addis, they entered the third Prochaska phase called "Preparation" in which a person intending to make change grapples with the practicalities of that change. They can feel deterred if they experience the resistance of others but on the other hand, if sure of themselves and well supported, they can also be strong role models for others by showing they are on board and buy in to the change.

Creating a new sense of identity

Francisco Varela, a Chilean biologist, neuroscientist and philosopher coined the term "Autopoiesis" (Maturana and Varela, 1988) which explains how a new identity was emerging in the group of 30 in the statement *"we are all in the same boat"*. Autopoiesis is how a living system maintains a continuing identity even as all its components are in continual flux, or how a cell *"bootstraps itself out of a soup of chemistry and physics"* (quoted in Goleman, 2003, p 306) and creates a boundary which represents both a separation and an identity. Varela described how any whole organism is more than the sum of its parts. Properties of the whole emerge which cannot be explained by the individual elements. He applies this to all levels of life from a single cell to the immune system, the mind, and even to whole communities.

Giving birth to the new "we"

In a healthy organisation, people feel a sense of significance and belonging: each department or team is simultaneously "well differentiated" – they know who they are – and "well integrated" – they are well linked with teams upon whom they depend (Oshry, 1996). A merger or change programme disrupts this.

Philip had experienced many times before the feeling of a real team around him but had been frustrated that it hadn't happened sooner in this case. Tony who has facilitated mergers of teams in many other situations (including hotels, hospitals, pharmaceuticals, finance and telecoms) knew how to produce a team from a collection of individuals but had also been surprised about how long it had taken to occur in this merger. Neither had taken sufficiently into account the challenges of distance, culture and the additional problems associated with the constant turnover of staff in the group.

Both of us had noticed there are special moments – in fact the true moment of a merger – when a team's new identity emerges like a protective bubble around a group of people.

There are three important things the leader can do to propel these aligning moments:

- *Share* the key information ("thing of beauty")
- *Challenge* the team to face the threat. When the problem starts to weigh heavily enough on a group of people they eventually unite around it. Provided they feel the trust of the leader in them, this expands their confidence.
- *Support* each person in the team to feel significant, competent and trusted (William Schutz 1994) including giving objective feedback on results and encouraging each person to build on these. When a person feels positive about who they are being (their personal "identity" in a group) this spills out positively in their behaviour towards others, making everyone in a group more confident and flexible.

If the leader encourages each person to make lateral connections with each colleague, and in this to discover how they can help each other in addressing the threat, then this multiplies the speed at which each person's frustration and fear transforms into courage and a sense of excitement.

Releasing passion

Larry Hirschhorn, a leading exponent of psychodynamic consulting, describes how the defensive patterns of an organisation arise through extreme anxiety or insufficient leadership and how the kind of passion expressed in the final Addis session is a way of unleashing positive energy and getting the organisation back on track (Hirschhorn, 1999).

An organisation answers the "what are we here for?" question with a "primary task". For Toyota it might be "to make and sell cars". In the case of this organisation it is "cultural relations". Any challenge to the way the Primary Task is delivered brings certain risks to staff – to their comfort, physical and psychological health, safety, relationships, prosperity and survival. The leader's job is to contain and spread this risk through clarity, certainty, rules and structure, so that staff can step up to responsibility and achieve a deep sense of engagement and fulfilment. If the risk is not properly contained then staff become overwhelmed with anxiety which they seek to contain through "social defences" (e.g. time-wasting, talking about easy topics instead of the real work, inflexibility, inefficient work processes).

When the Primary Task of an organisation changes from say, being an airline to a train operator or from being a "donor" to an "enterprise" organisation, then the risks entailed in changing provoke massive anxieties and social defences. Larry Hirshhorn points out that when people find passion in the new Primary Task, this gives a limitless source of energy, removing anxiety, unravelling social defences and providing a great capacity to endure difficulty.

■ What are the signs of progress in this phase?

1. When individuals are seriously preparing for change, grappling with the practicalities of "how?" rather than contemplating whether or not to go forward. Individuals are showing signs of commitment and the effect is spreading (Prochaska).
2. When the group is uniting against a common enemy or challenge (in this case "working on the regional budget") and starting to experience the strength and identity of the group (Varela).
3. When individuals and small groups find an action they are passionate to implement on behalf of the organisation (Hirschhorn).

■ What are the tools you can use?

In this third phase, the three tools which follow give the leader ways to engage others in addressing these key questions: *What information do we need to share? How will we take decisions and create accountability? How do we connect up across the team?*

No 1: "The Thing of Beauty"

The people who need to contribute to a team result need to know both the overall team result they are seeking to deliver and the contribution others expect from them. Initially, the shared task of the leadership community is something the leader knows a great deal about and may be somewhat burdened by. Their challenge is to find a way to express the shared task concisely in facts and detail and show individual members of the leadership community what they must contribute to produce the needed overall result.

In Addis, Philip and his Finance Director crafted a single sheet of paper which contained all the necessary information. This "Thing of Beauty" was then used by sub-groups to challenge and support each individual on how to make their contribution.

This clear, factual base to discussions made possible the change of heart in which members of the group of 30 discovered they were *"all in the same boat"*, interdependent and reliant on one another. Shortly afterwards, this led to "autopoiesis" and the sense of being one team.

No 2: The Steering Group

The people who take decisions need to be well-connected with those who have the key information as input into those decisions. After Douala, there was a yawning chasm between Philip and the group of 30. Philip expected the group of 30 to take decisions but they were showing no signs of being willing to do so.

As an interim measure, we engaged five members of the group of 30 (a mix of East and West, old and new) as a sounding board for Philip in setting the agenda and judging how hard to push on any particular point. Before the start of the Addis meeting and at the end of each day, the Steering Group met with Philip and the facilitators. This provided an opportunity to review progress and set priorities. At times, the Steering Group were able to take decisions and report back the following day thus spreading the leadership of the region beyond Philip into a slightly larger group as a step towards wider ownership by the group of 30.

No 3: Social mapping and swarms

Each person in a new team or network is a source of information for the others, yet it takes time and encouragement for connections to form. After Douala, we noticed the connections we expected between the 30 leaders had not yet materialised.

We asked them to count the number of meetings (face to face, telephone or email) they had held with colleagues in the group of 30 over the last six months. Then, they wrote the three figures on the flipchart and we could all see how many emails had been sent and how few phone calls they made. The powerful conclusion was "*we must pick the phone up and call each other more*". We then asked each person to draw their social map, first as an inner circle containing the three people of the 30 with whom they communicated most.

All members of the group went to stand in an open space with three long pieces of string, and handed the other ends to the three people in their inner circle. This showed us which individuals and which countries were the hubs through whom most communication went, and who was poorly connected on the periphery of the region. After this, we reflected on how many links are possible in a network of 30 (and we calculate the answer is 435!). The power of the network is realised when all those links are made. This showed people the potential of the team and how, by making more connections, everyone would benefit.

Finally, we enacted a moving simulation of a swarm (as in a flock of birds or shoal of fish) to represent a network of colleagues operating under two different conditions, the first supportive and the second hostile. Each person was to choose two others without letting them know. Under the first condition, they were to continue moving silently to maintain equidistance from their two people. This produced a gentle, powerful flowing and a joyful mood. Under the second condition, they were to choose two more people and to label one the bomb and the other the shield. They were to continue moving silently to keep themselves safe, with the shield always protecting them from the bomb. This time the movement was fast, jerky, exciting but chaotic and stressful. We reflected on the trustful style of relationships they needed to generate, in order for the team to be both enjoyable and highly productive.

■ What is the evidence of completing this phase?

- The leader feels relief and progress.
- The leadership community become united in a new identity, bonded, engaged and confident: "we know what we need to do".
- With the upward channel of communication open, the leadership community are ready to move the change out and down across their teams.

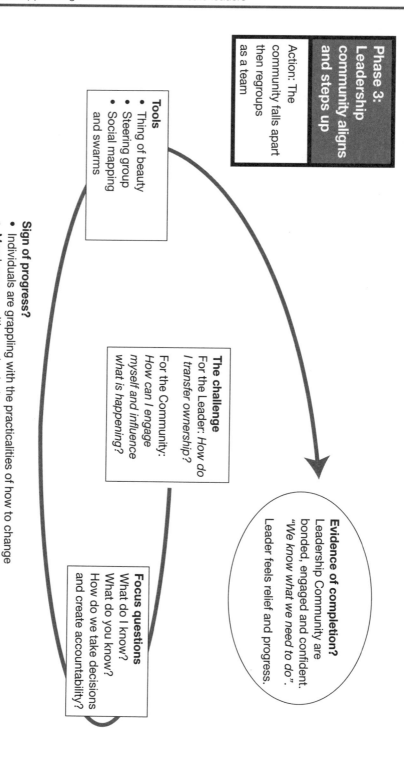

Phase 3:
Leadership
community aligns
and steps up

Action: The
community falls apart
then regroups
as a team

Tools
- Thing of beauty
- Steering group
- Social mapping
  and swarms

The challenge
For the Leader: *How do
I transfer ownership?*

For the Community:
*How can I engage
myself and influence
what is happening?*

Evidence of completion?
Leadership Community are
bonded, engaged and confident.
"We know what we need to do".
Leader feels relief and progress.

Focus questions
What do I know?
What do you know?
How do we take decisions
and create accountability?

Sign of progress?
- Individuals are grappling with the practicalities of how to change
- Members are uniting and enjoying the strength of the group
- Individuals find an action they are passionate to implement

Tips

- Acknowledge the progress you are making. Take a few minutes to recognise what has been achieved. But as a leader don't get seduced by the magic and relief of the breakthrough moments. What does the breakthrough tell you about the challenges ahead? What has not been resolved by the leap forward? What do you need to focus on next?
- Have some customer success stories up your sleeve to share with your team. It helps to demonstrate real progress on what really matters in your business – the customer. It helps the team focus on the outside world not just the anxieties of their internal change world. It's also good to share some failures. It makes the successes seem more credible and your team will appreciate the honesty.

Fourth phase: *People in the wider organisation pull back ... then embrace the new reality ...*

Fable Part 6

What the Chiefs least expected when they returned to their villages was to suffer the young chief's problem. Their people had lost confidence in them and rejected the call to change, saying: *"You have betrayed us and we no longer trust you"*.

Word had reached the young chief and from afar he stepped in. He asked each village to send a representative to a special meeting where the Chiefs would listen to the concerns of their people.

The people's representatives returned from this meeting saying: *"We have voiced our fears ... but the danger is real and it is not the fault of our leaders. They do not have all the answers and we must play our part in tackling this together"*.

With renewed faith the people were ready to plant the new seeds and fight back as one.

The Challenge

Suddenly it's as though the floodgates have opened. The leadership team buy in to the change and are enthusiastic to take it back to their teams. To their disappointment, their teams reject that call. The leaders' new enthusiasm leaves them cold, feeling betrayed and angry. How do we restore their confidence?

Philip: Our story

Since we had left Addis Ababa, Wambui's reflection on the way the leadership group was interacting was nagging away in my mind. It wouldn't go away. At the start of the merger, I had set out with the lofty intention of removing hierarchy and releasing the energy, commitment and capacity of the team of

500. Ensuring that the entire group understood and contributed to the future shape of the organisation was something I passionately believed in before taking over in East and West Africa. But thus far, I had only done this with smaller teams. I wasn't clear or confident how this would come about in so large a team spread across 4000 miles and 11 different countries. Nevertheless, I felt it was essential if we were to create a sustainable improvement in business performance.

For the previous 12 months, I had focused on engaging the leadership team – getting them to understand the need for change and trying to work through our different responses to the challenges in front of us. Tony and Ben, had helped me make a breakthrough in reaching that group of 30 and there was a growing feeling of joint purpose and team identity. After Addis, there was a real sense of elation in reaching a peak that we had been striving for. Now, I had this very real doubt about the strength of our achievement. Yes, my immediate leadership team were moving forward but was it far enough? And what about my wider team of 500? Where were they?

In travelling around the region, I wasn't convinced that we were communicating effectively on the change. Yes, in some countries you could see leaders were actively communicating with staff. For Otim this was a new responsibility:

"I had to do a presentation to all staff. There were some anxieties that jobs may be cut. We needed to reassure people and explain that it's good for us to work in a new way. Obviously some were sceptical and there wasn't 100% buy-in at the beginning. It took time to sit down with people and explain to them what it meant".

In some countries, effective communication was producing real improvements in delivery but often I could feel a resistance in staff or even a simple lack of knowledge on why the organisation was changing and what we were trying to achieve.

When I arrived in one country, staff used my visit to start a "work-to-rule" because of a dispute with management. Before I flew in, I had been forewarned by one of my close colleagues in Nairobi that this was likely to happen but worryingly, the country director was taken by surprise. On the way to the office from the airport, the country director was urgently ringing people to find out exactly what kind of action was being taken. When we got to the building all was quiet but staff were wearing black and red armbands as symbols of protest. It was a desperate effort to draw attention to their concerns and to the fact they feel their voice was simply not being heard. As I came down the stairs, I met a delegation sent to talk to me. It was intimidating and I felt slightly cross at being cornered in this way but, to defuse the situation, I suggested to the group that we convene an all staff meeting in an hour.

At the meeting, I simply sat and listened. I was clear that I was not promising to solve their issues at this point but I was willing to hear their concerns. As I visited the other offices in the operation, I repeated the same offer. Staff seemed glad of the opportunity for discussion and it succeeded in re-opening the potential for dialogue between management and staff. There was clearly a huge amount of hurt and misunderstanding on both sides.

Whilst this is an extreme example, it was symptomatic of communication problems I had noticed across the region, but overall my leadership team didn't agree. Then came a deafening wake-up call! In the annual staff survey carried out by MORI, the scores showing levels of confidence in our leadership have fallen significantly. It's a big disappointment but it confirms what I feared. Yes, the leadership team are on board but so far, we or they have failed to reach the wider staff back in countries. The worst result in the region is from our largest business – Nigeria – with 40% of the region's staff.

The truth is that in our heart of hearts, we have all known this issue was present but so far had left it in the background. Now, we had a great opportunity to get our team to look – as a group – at the issue of wider engagement. I could use our next leadership team meeting to raise some challenging questions. How do we engage the 500? How effectively do managers and staff relate to each other? What is it that blocks communication, that traps creativity and innovation? What is it that leaves people stuck in a cycle of low performance, productivity and dependency?

We had to get the problems – whatever they were – out on the table in order to spur the team into a new way of working. Yes, we could carry on as we were. It was certainly better than where we had started 12 months before but it was still far away from our vision of a high performance team. Alternatively, we now had the chance to press ahead through some very choppy waters towards another step change in performance. We chose to push on.

Working with Tony and my Head of Human Resources, we mobilised the 11 African members of the leadership team each to interview five staff from a cross-section of levels and departments in their own country to find out what makes them feel confident in their leaders and what gets in the way. We also asked the 11 Country Directors to interview three people asking the same question, and the Head of Human Resources to interview a handful of staff across the region. Through this approach, we reached 98 of the 500 staff – almost 20% of employees.

But what on earth would come up from this research and how would we be able to deal with it? Was this going to be our Pandora's box? The issues were deeply sensitive: not only were we talking about relationships between country directors and their teams, there were also issues between UK-appointed and African staff. We knew as a British organisation working in Africa, we had the legacy of the UK's colonial past to negotiate. The biggest cop out would have been to avoid the sensitive issues but confronting them meant entering a minefield where we needed to be "inclusive" and hyper-aware of the pitfalls that arise from engaging in difficult conversations across cultures, about race and between groups and individuals in different positions of power. We mustn't fall into the trap of generalising or stereotyping. It would have been much easier to avoid all this, leaving in place the barriers to performance. While carefully designing our approach to the coming meeting, we consulted closely with our organisation's Equal Opportunities and Diversity Unit based in the UK.

The meeting was due to take place in Lagos, a chaotic megalopolis of around 8 million people in Nigeria. It's a place of high energy, of charged emotions, where people speak their mind, tempers flare quickly and just as quickly quieten down again. It was the perfect metaphor for the days ahead. Although we were staying in an international hotel, major rebuilding works were going on next door to our meeting room and our conversations took place against the noisy backdrop of drilling. Twice, water pipes burst in the ceiling overhead filling an empty champagne bucket put there for the purpose, and breaking the tension by causing welcome laughter amongst the group.

So how did we choose to address Wambui's question on senior management participation in the meeting? Tony and I took the controversial decision to split the group for a day – country directors in one room, other senior managers in the other. It was a risk. Would it reinforce the divisions that were already there? How would this be interpreted by the two different groups? Would it alienate country directors?

We felt it was a risk worth taking. Wambui's feedback had hit home – hard. We wanted to get staff voice into the room without distortion and without being suppressed by the more experienced and influential country director group. We knew we had to build the capacity of the less senior members of staff if they were to have genuine influence on the meeting. If they didn't have that influence, we would simply not be able to move to a new level of performance as a team.

With the African senior manager group, we spent a day looking at the research. What did it tell us? They took turns to share their findings from each country with their colleagues and as people listened to each other the experience was empowering. As Binte from Senegal said:

"I kept asking myself 'here am I standing in front of colleagues and they see me as someone they can seek guidance from'. It helped build my capacity".

How could this group best present the messages back to the country directors? The group had not only found many common issues but also the courage and determination to present their findings clearly and in a balanced way. They were not naïve: while knowing this was a unique opportunity to expose the real issues, they risked an adverse reaction and needed to plan carefully what to say. All played a part.

Meanwhile country directors worked on the issues blocking our ability to deliver the change programme. When we came back together, the country directors surprised the African senior managers by presenting an imaginative and playful analysis of the challenges we were facing in our capacity to deliver. They made a clear commitment to communicate the vision, clarify expectations, bring resources, create openness and empower staff. They underlined that failure to do this would ultimately mean closure, while on the other hand success would enable everyone to deliver relevant programmes and interesting jobs. So far, so good.

Then it was the turn of the African senior manager group to feedback. The session that followed was uncomfortable. You could hear a pin drop. For the first time, the whole group including country directors were really listening well. The feedback was direct, personal and emotionally charged. It started positively. The African senior managers first point was that they valued the vision, the sense of direction and the willingness to work as a team to address the points they were about to raise. Then Foluke from Cameroon, stood up to communicate staff concerns. This was her first leadership team meeting and, initially shy, she soon found her voice in giving feedback to the leadership team on issues which were personal and highly contentious:

"You seem indifferent, aloof. You don't say hello. You don't reply to emails. In short, it feels like you lack respect for us".

"You are secretive, you fail to consult, and present decisions badly. In short, we feel taken for granted".

"You overload the capable staff and condone poor performance".

"We need to modernise the management-staff relationship from one which feels like master-servant to one of two-way, mutual accountability, with feedback in both directions".

"On pay and conditions we need rigour, transparency and staff involvement".

Foluke's clear and objective delivery of these points contributed to the deeper shift in the leaders' attitudes and behaviour which was to follow.

Next the country directors were asked to respond. There was silence and it was clear they had very mixed emotions. Quite a number were simply stunned. For the African senior managers, there was a sense of exhilaration as some of their most deeply felt concerns were finally expressed. They had finally won the attention of the country directors and their voice was fully present in the room.

Instead of provoking a bun fight, we decided to pair up each country director with the senior African manager colleague from their own country, to review the findings, identify and explore in greater depth exactly which aspects applied to them. We could see that some pairs were getting straight down to this whilst others were having difficulties. One country director simply avoided sitting with his colleague! Another bursting with anger told Tony this approach had been *"wrong"* and *"too negative"*: *"I felt doors slamming in my face"*. Blinded by a red mist, he failed to notice that he was talking all about himself while his country colleague, an African senior manager, was ignored, sitting patiently beside him waiting for the storm to pass.

After the allotted time, the country directors asked to be given the chance to respond as a group.

There was a hush in the room. One country director simply thanked the country-appointed staff for what they had said, acknowledged the importance of the issues and asked for time to consider his response. Others were uncomfortable with the emotional nature of the discussion and tried to depersonalise and rationalise what they were hearing. Anthony, for example, stood up and said something like:

"I can see what you're saying. Actually, there is a taxonomy of behaviours here and I think I can see a new model of leadership that we can draw up".

Francis, on the other hand, was clearly angry and not liking what he was hearing. He started to question the process:

"Hang on – where did you get this information from? Why is it confidential? I'm not sure any of it's true anyway and I think presenting it anonymously in this way is simply unfair to us".

Although the country directors had asked for the floor, finding themselves under the spotlight in this way was a lot to cope with. The conversation lurched unpredictably between hurt feelings and clumsy attempts to recover.

A long, meandering but moving discussion followed with the African members of the team telling stories from their research about the impact of leader behaviour, highlighting cultural differences for example in the way people say "hello". People were bursting to speak but the individual contributions didn't connect with each other, as though each person was on their own with their emotions, venting and thrashing around. The conversation became frustrating to listen to and it looked as if Tony was finding it tiring to facilitate. On the positive side, people were no longer finding clever ways to reject the findings, but were now struggling as if to digest some exotic, unknown food. While in each case the speaker was earnest, they were not yet a team taking responsibility. An hour passed and the conversation still had life but it was not clear where it was going.

The most heartfelt issue was the paralysing effect of decisions and conversations avoided, particularly those that relate to staff who were not performing. But above all, what worried me as the conversation went on was that a chasm seemed to be opening in the room leaving the African members of the team as victims of a bad former colonial power. Then Yahya from West Africa proposed a practical action that began to heal the rift:

"If a director phoned a few people up to speak to them personally they would be so delighted, so confident and he could have so many supporters!"

Mark, a country director from East Africa, seized the moment and built a bridge with his honest disclosure:

"I know how bad some of you feel, because I've also felt badly treated by the organisation at various points over the years".

This surprising contribution drew the group together again in common cause.

As the afternoon came to a close, things still felt inconclusive and "up in the air", and in the goldfish bowl atmosphere of the meeting I found myself exasperated. I felt that we still seemed to be avoiding some of the issues. Ben was exploding with impatience wanting to blow up the entire group and this was when we nicknamed him "Mr Dynamite"! Tony who had been holding the space as facilitator for the entire afternoon was exhausted, but seemed to accept the need for people to vent and explore before taking responsibility. Despite the frustrations, he was confident all was OK, but he was wrung out, and seemed barely able to continue speaking! With strong emotions still swirling around everyone needed time to reflect – often in private and not just overnight but in the days and weeks ahead.

The next day we asked each country director to work with their senior managers in country "pairs" thinking through plans for how they should respond to the feedback in their country operations, and how they would communicate the discussion with their teams. We also completed a quite different topic on prioritising our key stakeholders, which served to switch everyone's attention back out of introspection into the external delivery challenges we faced.

In a coffee break, Tony and I were relieved to see new and spontaneous mixing amongst the group with different clusters forming instead of the usual obvious cliques. Tony told me conversations seemed more open, and he noticed that it was easier to draw ripples of laughter from the group. Personal chats with a few people had taught him more about previously unmentioned challenges faced by staff including the difficulty of speaking about their personal performance, the isolation of the country director role, and what to do if you receive death threats while introducing a new company purchasing system! We had succeeded in bringing skeletons out of the cupboard and there was no going back now. We could expect the word about this meeting to spread fast to all staff and success now depended on the leaders showing they had listened and changed their behaviour.

In spite of the difficulty of the conversations, this meeting was a critical step in getting all senior managers to a common understanding of the issues and barriers to engaging **all** staff in the change process. As Otim, an African senior manager says:

"This open and frank discussion led to change in the way people behaved and the assumptions they made which I thought was extremely positive. It opened the way for us to work together, irrespective of who you are and it created a fundamental and positive impact for the region".

During the course of the meeting Ian, one of the country directors, had picked up some strong and affecting stories:

"It revealed an awful lot actually about some things that needed to be uncovered: directors who went into their office and never said 'hello' to people, some people feeling they had to kind of psyche themselves up for 15 minutes in their car before getting out of it and going into work. So there were some really quite deep issues of morale and feeling amongst some staff that through a brave move Philip unearthed and those issues could then be talked about and dealt with".

In my closing remarks at Lagos, I took the opportunity to thank Ian, who was due to move back to the UK, for his significant contribution to the region's work over the previous 18 months. Ian's support in the early part of the merger had been vital, both for his practical work in reducing the product range, and for his personal support helping to enrol West African and smaller countries into the new enlarged region. Spontaneously and with real affection, the others in the leadership team responded to my few words with a standing ovation leaving Ian shuffling from foot to foot in embarrassment.

This poignant moment marked the end of an era in this team's life. We had just made a difficult crossing and having got safely to the other side, now we had to say goodbye to someone who had helped get us there. Ian's hard work on all our behalves had been appreciated by everyone and he had the respect of the entire team. It made me reflect on the key qualities I valued in Ian and other colleagues in positions of authority over the years. It seemed to boil down to this: integrity, commitment and service to the group rather than the self. All of these had come to inform my sense of what a leader could and should do.

Looking back, the meeting had exposed senior managers, both country directors and their African colleagues to staff opinion. This helped UK colleagues to better understand the cultural context to the feedback and to start thinking through how they could work together to engage staff. The process also empowered the African managers and encouraged them to take joint responsibility for responding to staff views. This was a major step in getting our teams to work together to address deeply felt and long-standing barriers to change. Yahya used a word picture to describe how important this meeting had been for keeping all members of the leadership team together:

"When the river is travelling downstream you have to be careful to ensure that the front water does not separate from the back water. When this starts to happen before long the stream dries up. It's as simple as that. So you make sure you carry everyone, all members of the teams, along together".

Otim describes how this meeting finally brought African senior managers on a par with their UK counterparts, creating new opportunities for them to lead change in the region:

"Previously it wasn't recognised for us to sit on senior management teams and things like that. But now we do have, as we speak, a number of senior management posts that have been created across the region and staff who can contribute at that level actually filling those posts. That was something very positive that came out of that meeting. We recognised what we can do together as a region that can create impact and also we learnt that we've got talent in the region. It doesn't matter if you're African staff or UK-appointed, we can contribute equally together and create impact. We removed some real and serious divides between African and UK-appointed staff."

Word spread quickly amongst staff about the conversations that had taken place at our meeting and the commitments to change from management. This was the opening of a door. You do not change 70 years of working practice overnight but Lagos was a symbolic ending of an old way of relating. It gave me as the leader, a platform on which to hold others accountable to a new way of working and through some simple behavioural changes on the part of the leadership team, confidence in our leadership increased significantly. In the global staff survey undertaken by MORI the following year, our results were not only the best in our organisation but also matched figures of top ten performing companies both private and public sector in the UK. This included extremely high positive ratings for statements such as:

- I have confidence in the management team running my country
- Staff are consulted. Change is well managed. I am informed.
- I am aware of improvements arising from the last survey.
- I understand the contribution I am expected to make.
- Training and development is helping me to develop skills I need in my job.

Although we had taken a risk with our approach to this meeting, it had paid off, finally delivering a fundamental shift in the way we worked together as a team.

■ How do you approach this phase?

The story of this stage in the change process is particularly challenging. As in the fable, the Chiefs had gone back home and been rejected by their people who felt betrayed. Observing this had happened, Philip wondered how he could form a "distance repair" without disabling the Chiefs and making things worse between them and their people. How do you successfully bring difficult and emotionally charged issues to the attention of senior managers? And, even more tricky, how do you get them to engage positively with these issues when they potentially challenge their sense of humanity and integrity in dealing with others?

The power of stories

We wanted researchers to gather stories and to use these to unearth the issues that needed to be addressed. While working at the World Bank, Stephen Denning tells how through trial and error, he discovered and developed storytelling in order to galvanise the organisation's knowledge management activities (Denning, 2004). Denning educated himself in how others, from Aristotle onwards, have used storytelling. He was particularly interested in discovering the narrative power of a traditional story and its limitations in the context of an organisation. Some stories are boring, some need to be open to provoke people to think, some need to be upbeat and positive to motivate, while others are powerful because they are unashamedly negative, and illuminate a problem that needs addressing. Inspired by Denning, we designed the research to collect both positive and negative stories.

Reconciliation of interests

Nevertheless, we were concerned that as people received negative stories during the workshop they might start to feel sorry for themselves – feeling unloved when they receive criticism, or incompetent, or badly looked after by their organisation – and that they might collapse again into victim mode. Alternatively, they might swing into over-compassion for staff and fail in their duty to the organisation. We needed a way to call people to their responsibility as leaders recognising both their accountability to the organisation and to their individual members of staff. Charles Handy, one of the leading thinkers and writers on organisations, defines leadership as "*combining the interests of individuals with the collective interests of the larger community to which they belong"* (Handy, 2008). The effective leader needs to reconcile those interests if the organisation is to succeed. Understanding those interests and achieving this balance, is a central leadership dilemma and one that leaders need to resolve in each decision they take. We shared Charles Handy's definition as we introduced the workshop and carried it as a reference point as we facilitated the discussion constantly asking ourselves: are both sides of the leadership dilemma being expressed in the room right now and how are they coming together?

Having difficult conversations

We anticipated that after the stories had been presented, and the country pairs had worked together on the feedback, there would be a need for a large group conversation in which the whole plenary made sense of the sometimes difficult topics being raised and the larger process of change they found themselves in. But what sort of conversation did we need to have and how should we facilitate this?

David Bohm, a leading quantum physicist, later in his life devoted himself to the practice of "dialogue". He distinguished "dialogue" from simple "discussion" which he likened to a ping-pong match in which we hit a ball back and forth between us, normally with a purpose to win and only occasionally accepting part of another person's point of view (Bohm, 1990). The purpose of dialogue is to come together as colleagues, going beyond one person's understanding, suspending assumptions, embracing contradictions and confusion, and achieving a common meaning. The focus is bringing to the surface and altering the tacit infrastructure of thought.

Bill Isaacs and Peter Senge working at Massachusetts Institute of Technology (MIT) have built on Bohm's work to turn dialogue into a practical method. They find such conversations go through various crises, or "hot moments", where extreme views provoke distress in others (Isaacs, 1999). Provided people pay attention without falling victim to their strong inner reactions, then they are able to reach a deep "crisis of collective pain" in which thinking takes on a different slower pace, with a deeper sense of connection. Out of this connection, new solutions emerge and become possible. Central to the success of dialogue is what Bill Isaacs describes as "the container", which means creating a setting that is sufficiently safe and clear so that it is possible for participants to discuss a topic that is dangerous. Tony and Ben's role in providing this container was critical. As Ian, one of the country directors, emphasises:

> *"In terms of getting commitment from people and bringing them together, Tony and Ben's facilitation was useful in that process. It would've been more difficult for Philip to do it by himself or for us to do it, so it was critical to have external facilitation".*

Actions speak volumes

When the whole group dialogue in Lagos had reached its natural conclusion, we asked country pairs to identify behaviours and actions they needed to take on their return to their workplaces. Most people were tired. Some were quite disorientated and concerned about the quality of the action plans they were preparing. We asked ourselves what we should be looking for from our leadership team. John Kotter says:

> *"Deeds speak volumes. When you say one thing and do another, cynical feelings can grow exponentially... The guiding team says we too are being asked to change and, like you we won't get it right immediately, we need your help and support.... people love honesty, it makes them feel safer"* (Kotter, 2002).

This is what we needed from our team – simple and highly visible behavioural changes coming out of the meeting that would signal with bright lights, bells and whistles blowing, that something positive has happened and a shift has occurred.

■ What are the signs of progress in this phase?

1. When staff members bring both positive stories (demonstrating confidence and support for their leaders) and negative stories (indicating a lack of fear and a desire to create conditions for success) to their leaders (Denning).

2. When all in the leadership community understand the organisation's purpose, how they can contribute to and benefit from success (Charles Handy).

3. When the difficult interpersonal issues are out on the table and the different experiences and expectations of individual members are heard and in doing so, the group strive collectively to overcome the issues raised (Isaacs and Senge).

4. When the leadership community commit to simple actions and behaviours that will build confidence and respect in the workplace (Kotter).

■ What are the tools you can use?

In this fourth phase, the three tools which follow give the leader ways of engaging others in addressing these key questions: *What do you want from me? What do I want from you?* To be more specific: *What leader behaviour helps or hinders staff confidence? What issues do leaders need their colleagues to hear? What simple improvement actions and behaviours will leaders commit to?*

No 1: The staff research

Following the staff survey, we needed to find a means for staff to raise their real concerns and to have these addressed by their leaders. However, staff felt insecure and concerned that they might pay a heavy price for speaking out. We designed research which protected confidentiality and encouraged honesty.

Each member of the leadership team interviewed between three and five members of staff in their country. We provided questions and a format for the interviews covering:

1. Examples of behaviour that give you confidence in the leader
2. Examples of behaviour that take away confidence from the leader
3. What good things your leaders are doing already
4. What you would like your leaders to do more of or less of
5. How could you step up yourself as a leader to provide a more positive environment for others?

After the staff research, we brought together the African senior managers for a full day to analyse common themes, find their voice and prepare to present the findings back to Country Directors.

No 2: The stories – talking in the round

The staff research and feedback left the Country Directors feeling criticised and they wanted the "right to reply". So, we arranged 11 chairs in a circle and the rest of the group sat round the edge. The Country Directors were invited to hold a conversation amongst themselves in the presence of the wider leadership team. After initial comments from each country director this became a very open dialogue involving the whole group of 30. One person spoke at a time while 29 people listened intently, both to the words and to their deeper inner reactions. The facilitator's role was simply to receive contributions from individuals, giving them time to say what was important until after about two hours the dialogue naturally came to a close. This provided the opportunity for people to get things off their chests, to explain past misunderstandings, some of them culturally based (e.g. *"you might think when a Nigerian says 'hello' a second time he is simple – this is not the case…"*). The session rebuilt the relationship between Country Directors and their African senior managers, and afterwards sent ripples out to the wider staff. Afterwards, the team conversations were more two way, more "in the same boat as fellow human beings" with less hierarchy or formality.

No 3: The action plans

Following talking in the round, we thought it important for each country to commit to an action plan that would both communicate the research findings to local staff and put in place the necessary corrective actions. Country pairs were to spend the final hour completing an action plan with a named person responsible and date beside each of the following:

1. Circulate research findings to all staff
2. A personal response thanking each interviewee
3. A "stepping forwards" meeting of the country management team
4. An all staff meeting reporting back from Lagos
5. A feedback meeting for each leader with their direct reports
6. A change committee in each office
7. A regional vision workshop including progress to date and gaps to close

■ What is the evidence of completing this phase?

- Staff have spoken out on issues that concern them and the leadership community have actively listened.

- Leaders have got over the feeling of *"you don't love us any more, we're angry with you"* and come to a point where they recognise *"we need you if as an organisation we're going to survive"*.
- The leadership community have identified how their own behaviour is an obstacle to staff engagement.
- Staff recognise that they and the leadership are *"in the same boat"*. They have moved from mistrust to a recognition that *"you are in a difficult position too"*.
- Leaders and staff commit to specific positive behaviours that they are prepared to sustain e.g. saying 'hello', knowing people's names, explaining decisions and raising issues constructively.

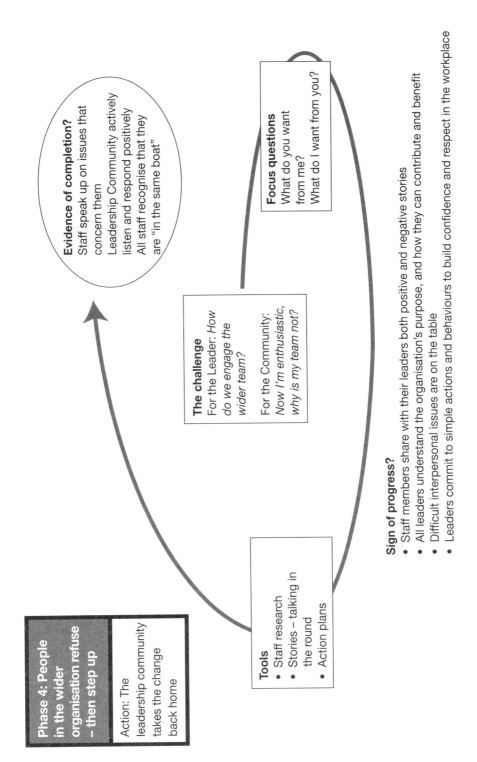

Phase 4: People in the wider organisation refuse – then step up

Action: The leadership community takes the change back home

Evidence of completion?
Staff speak up on issues that concern them
Leadership Community actively listen and respond positively
All staff recognise that they are "in the same boat"

Focus questions
What do you want from me?
What do I want from you?

The challenge
For the Leader: *How do we engage the wider team?*

For the Community: *Now I'm enthusiastic, why is my team not?*

Tools
• Staff research
• Stories – talking in the round
• Action plans

Sign of progress?
• Staff members share with their leaders both positive and negative stories
• All leaders understand the organisation's purpose, and how they can contribute and benefit
• Difficult interpersonal issues are on the table
• Leaders commit to simple actions and behaviours to build confidence and respect in the workplace

Tips

- There is a serious risk that the bad news from staff turns off your senior managers. They become defensive and/or try and avoid the issues. Give people time to digest. Make sure your influencers in the group know what is coming. Make sure managers have room to respond. Facilitators need to manage this carefully.
- Action plans don't need details but simplicity and heartfelt commitment.
- Dealing with management–staff issues is a sensitive area. Make sure that those with responsibility for Equal Opportunities and Diversity in your organisation are aware of what you are doing and seek their support and advice.

Fifth phase: *Identity shifts and the rubber hits the road!*

Fable Part 7

As they started to work together – chiefs and villagers, East and West – a remarkable thing happened. The villagers looked at their reflection in the lake and the Chiefs were no longer thick-skinned like hippos. They were no longer divided between East and West and the people were no longer blind. They had been magically transformed.

What had they become? Not slow elephants, nor tall giraffes, nor crafty hyenas, but animals that were faster and more cooperative. The Chiefs said *"we have become like gazelles"*, and the people happily responded: *"Yes we are lean, adaptable, and ready to run energetically together to find the best pastures"*.

Since that day there has been a new confidence, with women and smaller tribes also contributing their voices alongside others. The people suffer less as they face up to reality, create solutions together and are leaders influencing each other. The young chief is no longer needed and has moved on to be a chief in another land.

This story of hippos, lions and gazelles is now told to all the young gazelle children and acted out in their games. Before adulthood, each child learns how to turn themselves into a lion and how to deal with any territorial hippos they might meet, just in case.

The Challenge

There is a new sense of excitement, possibility and achievement. We're being recognised for our success in introducing change. With people on-board we now have an opportunity to raise the bar and tackle some long-standing and ultimately life-threatening issues. How can we engage the whole team and realise their full potential in addressing these issues?

Philip: Our story

Things are really starting to move! During the last six months, the wider team of 500 has really come together and there is a noticeable sense of team identity built on the successful delivery of a range of ambitious new products that are recognised as having potential in the wider world beyond our region. The staff survey figures have vindicated the risks we took in Lagos and have boosted the confidence of the leadership group.

Just before our last team meeting in Lagos, I received a request in feedback from staff to write a regular monthly email updating them on progress we are making across the region and how we are tackling the challenges facing us. I had resisted doing this before, feeling that somehow I would be adopting a leadership pose and "voice" that wasn't my own. But since the feedback was honestly and bravely given I feel I should respond. So, for the last six months, I've been writing a short monthly message to all staff and it surprises me how positive the response is. I ask people to get in touch if they want to comment on issues or ask questions and amazingly, some do. It seems to reduce the distance between us, bringing the East and West Africa team together within its new identity. It reflects me finding a stronger voice as a leader.

We also introduced a recognition scheme across the region. Every three months, we give cash prizes to members of the team who have helped us to deliver on our change plans. The scheme was set up so that over the year, we can expect 25% of staff to receive bonuses and recognition for their contribution to our work. Every three months, an email goes out to all staff announcing the winners and describing how they helped us to deliver change. There is huge enthusiasm from staff for this initiative and I get lots of emails from winners saying how excited they are at being named and how it is inspiring them to do more.

All this told me we were in a strong position. We are delivering a new level of performance and impact, as Otim, one of the African senior managers describes:

> "'One customer said to me the other day 'I've known your organisation for many years from the tinniest little thing to this huge thing'. That was his comment but we've never changed numbers: we've always been less than 25 people in the office … but his perception of our organisation is that we have become this big thing, doing a lot more!'"

There is a sense of unity and purpose across the business and I'm starting to think "we've got momentum that is coming from all parts of the organisation not being pushed by me". For the first time, I feel that the leadership team of 30 is really confident and secure in its role. As Akello says:

> *"Myself I feel like I'm more empowered to do things because I now have that challenge of saying "I must prove to myself that I'm able to do this" and I'm always looking for the best result I can produce".*

The leaders are trusted to act by their teams and by me as regional director. This in turn gives them a strong licence to operate. I could easily just let this carry on under its own steam. What exactly is there for us to do now?

It's going through my mind that time is running out for me as a leader of this group. I probably had eighteen months left in the job and I'm wondering *"am I satisfied with where we've got to? Have I really achieved what we needed to?"* I'm also asking *"what on earth should I do after that eighteen months? What is the next challenge for me?"* With these questions in mind, I ask Tony for some leadership coaching to help me clarify next steps.

Shortly, after one of these coaching sessions, I'm sitting in a taxi on the way to work. It suddenly comes to me as a flash of inspiration. I'm struck by the fact that whilst we've made some very significant changes, particularly in developing a strong product range and engaging the team across the region, we haven't yet taken the opportunity to address some of the deeper, underlying issues that hold us back as an organisation.

I know the team is much more receptive to new ideas and ready to engage with them. Why not use the new found energy, confidence and commitment of this group as an opportunity to radically redraw the boundaries of our organisation? This is a chance not just for a series of incremental shifts but for a big leap forward.

That morning, I work with some of my colleagues to come up with some new default positions for the organisation – a set of 10 givens – simple descriptions of how we will operate going forwards. The idea is that with these we will draw a line in the sand, delineating the shift between the old and the new worlds of our organisation. We then have a brainstorming session on what we think are the few significant areas of challenge for us as an organisation. We end up with six. These include reviewing our business model, expanding our customer base, demonstrating the impact of our work, and improving levels of customer service. There is a wonderful sense of energy in the room and amazingly, this is the work of just a few hours.

Some days later, I ring Tony and tell him that this is what I want us to focus on in the next leadership meeting – harnessing the new-found belief and enthusiasm of the East and West Africa team to understand and respond to these six big challenges facing the organisation. The leadership team will redefine the way the East and West Africa business operates and delivers. It is a chance for them to really lead the change. If we pull it off, we will finally be delivering leadership across and down through the team. Weeks before the meeting, we ask the leadership team to organise themselves into one of the six challenge areas that appeals to their interest and strengths.

When we get to the meeting in Dar-Es-Salaam, Tanzania, we find we are staying in an incredibly beautiful hotel overlooking the harbour. We have a meeting room with natural light. There is a great bar on the eighth floor. People are in an excellent mood and there is a real sense of pleasure at being back together again. This is evident in the first session where we review our journey as a team over the last two years. Emotions of pride, sometimes surprise, at how far we've come as a group, and a strong sense of identity emerge. This is palpable for the new members coming into this team for the first time.

We have planned to ask each of the six challenge groups to find their passion for tackling their challenge area, to work out what the most difficult issue and core dilemma is, to describe the step change that we want to achieve and then to agree two actions that they will take responsibility for delivering over the next six months making themselves accountable to the Leadership Community.

On the first day, Tony and Ben keep reminding us of the need for equal voice and they seem to have stepped up a gear with dynamic plenaries that draw more and more energy from the group. It feels like a convection current of positive power that is building up within the team. As the day comes to a close, we are upbeat. Then, unexpectedly, while a few of us are reviewing the day, a strange argument breaks out between two country directors, Chris from Sierra Leone and Gail from Ethiopia,. Chris is concerned:

> "Let's be honest, what we're doing here is a sham! After this meeting, the African senior managers all go back into a hierarchy. We are pretending we are empowering them but not really. What are we empowering them with?"

Gail who had previously confided her frustrations with the rough and tumble of our earlier meetings ("*although I was allowed to speak, I was not really listened to*") bursts out in frustration:

"It is patronising and untrue to say we are not working as equals. Just look at the reality of those African senior managers who are taking on team leader roles on behalf of the group. What do they say? Just look and listen to the evidence. Our people out there are seeing and feeling the difference on the ground!"

The exchange touched a nerve and took us briefly back to the issues of Lagos. At first I felt a bit anxious about the strength of these emotions but as the discussion continued, it became clear that actually Gail and Chris were in violent agreement.

Chris's concern was based on a fear that what he was seeing grow in this meeting – passion, commitment, confidence across the team – would simply evaporate once we returned to our offices. Although he sounded sceptical, it was as though he was checking-in with others on their levels of commitment. Gail, who was finding the meeting liberating for her and her senior manager, fervently wanted to hold on to something that was clearly working for her. In speaking up with such enthusiasm, Gail was able to reassure Chris that the commitments we had made in Lagos were shared, deeply held and sincere. Thankfully, the following day, progress continued and Gail told Tony how far the team had come since she joined in Addis:

"At first I felt there was no space for me in a leadership team dominated by men, but now this feeling is totally gone".

As the team continued to look at the core dilemmas confronting the organisation, we were brought face to face with the uncomfortable truth of having no easy options. Tony and Ben were really pushing the group not to gloss over the issues but to take time to understand them deeply and to make sure the whole leadership team understood the problem well enough to be receptive to any solutions they came up with later. For some, this was too slow and they wanted to move on because they felt the issues were obvious. But getting people to connect profoundly to the problems is an essential part of focusing their energy to solving them.

Just when things seem to be going very well, Tony and Ben hit us with an uncomfortable question: *"what makes a person most influential in this team?"* They ask us to stand in order of how much influence each of us feels we have on this group. We shuffle around a bit and settle in a semi-circle with me (as Regional Director) feeling rather on my own at the high influence end. What followed was interesting. First, we talked a bit about why people were standing where they were standing. I learned that many felt just as uncomfortable as me having this hierarchy of influence exposed so starkly. Then shockingly, in spite of all our progress since Lagos someone noticed how uneven the circle was. And, yes, when you looked it was true: those near to me were more likely to be from the East, male, white, UK-appointed... and the proportions shifted as you went round.

Suddenly and worryingly, we were returning to Chris's concerns of the night before. Then, as we began to explore this circle of influence with the group, Otim from Kenya and Sanyu from Tanzania, two African senior managers, who had been in the middle of the circle, spontaneously walked to join me at the high influence end. Otim declared to everyone:

"Sanyu and I just talked and said 'we know what we need to do and we are not going to wait for others'. We have decided to put all of our energy behind the work that we are doing in this workshop and we recognise we have a real opportunity to influence the big decisions the region is taking. It is up to us to take that chance. That is why we are moving".

Immediately standing next to these two colleagues I felt much less lonely. Again the expectation and sense of hierarchy was challenged from within the group. Taking the cue from Sanyu and Otim, Tony concluded the session by asking each of us to figure out how we can both influence others more and also allow ourselves to be influenced by others. We discuss this in groups for five minutes before continuing with our task.

While this had not been comfortable the exercise had exposed a number of powerful points. First, it reminded us of the risk of complacency creeping into a team when you think you have tackled some difficult tasks. For us, this was particularly true around issues of equality of voice. There was always the risk that inequality drifts back into our way of working through laziness or lack of attention. Second, Otim and Sanyu had shown us how individuals need to take their chance to create influence. Once again, team members had shown courage and woken the rest of us up to our responsibility.

For the rest of the afternoon, we keep going back into plenary in order to get whole group buy-in to the different directions we might take. Each challenge group then has to trust the other challenge groups to do work on their behalf. This last part is a particular challenge. Too often in the past, senior managers were blocking actions across the region because they felt they had not been closely involved in the decision-making process. Given the size of the region and the challenges we faced, the team needed to accept that it was impossible for all of us to be involved in decisions in all areas. Colleagues would need to work on issues on the organisation's behalf. If they were to be effective and empowered in doing this, all of us (including me as Regional Director) needed to give up some of our authority and let them get on with the work. This is why we spent so much time on the sign-off process for proposals made by the challenge groups throughout the meeting.

The tone of the meeting continued to be challenging but positive. Then, suddenly we hit another snag. One sub-group, over-confident from the positive reception to some of their earlier ideas, misjudged the mood of the team and suggested a "big bang" approach to staff change that left the meeting angry. Their ideas were rejected as "arrogant" and "bullshit". Three amazing things happen. First, the sub-group gets this feedback very directly from the wider team. Second, they show incredible strength in taking that feedback constructively. They go back, rethink and re-present their ideas taking into account the views of the leadership team. Third, the leadership team as a whole shows emotional maturity and a collective sense of responsibility by consciously making sure that the sub-group are drawn back into the leadership team as a whole and don't feel left behind. There is an added sense of solidarity as a result and watching this take place, I almost want to jump up and down, I feel so proud to head up this organisation!

As the days go by, the sense of momentum is growing. It's like we've moved into fifth gear after having been stuck in second for a long while. There is joint action, responsibility and purpose in the room. Everyone seems to be engaged, sleeves rolled up addressing the challenges and their new tasks.

As the Dar meeting draws to a close instead of being tired people seem inspired, more confident than ever that they can rise to the challenge. There is a palpable shift in the identity of the group of 30 as they recognise themselves contributing in new, more significant ways and with a renewed sense of purpose. It's as though we all grow a bit taller, proud of ourselves and what we are achieving.

Tony and Ben ask the group of 30 to describe who they have been this week. Almost for the first time, they recognise their power, authority and responsibility as they say:

> *"We have been leaders not managers because we have been decision-makers, focused, critical and challenging, inclusive, taking responsibility, listening, evaluating, empowered and setting policy".*

By the end of the meeting, the burden is shifting from me as leader to the leadership community as a whole. When I convene the Steering Group for a post-meeting review I am bowled over by their enthusiasm. Mark says we "*got to clarity*". Thomas says "*we are suddenly in the business of being a region*". Gail says "*for the first time I feel we're going back with the tools we need to work with*". And it was Chris, who three days earlier had been worried that this was "a sham", whose attitude was transformed:

> "*I have seen genuine empowerment and while I am still sceptical – that is my nature – I feel what you could almost call enthusiasm, I almost want to burst out in delight…!*"

Chris paused mid-sentence as if to recover himself and we moved on to agree on the message and next steps we would take away.

Many of us attending the meeting are leaving on the same plane out of Dar-Es-Salaam and the mood is buoyant. Mark, enjoying his new-found clarity, is reflecting on how this new sense of alignment has been created:

> "*We don't have a grand strategy that will fix everything. Instead of setting out to answer a very big question with a very big answer that doesn't really work, we start out with that very big question but then you start producing a whole series of incremental answers that move you forwards, keeping you flexible as you go. That is the right way to develop an organisation*".

We take off over the Indian Ocean and head north to Nairobi passing over the snow covered, Mount Kilimanjiro. I later see this scene played out on a video that had been made of our meeting. It looks great! It's certainly never been easier to write my monthly all-staff email reporting on what we have achieved. I sign it off:

> "*I was inspired by the willingness and ability of the leadership team to take responsibility for leading us forward in meeting the challenges we face and to do so quickly and decisively*".

Following this meeting, I hear more positive reports. For example Otim reflected his excitement at the role he was now playing having decided to put all his energy into being a positive influencer:

> "*Now, just picture this scenario: I am a locally appointed member of staff and I'm meeting country directors who are senior to me, and this team of country directors and regional people who are way above me, but I am leading them and getting them to do work to address income levels in the region!*"

Akello, who in Nairobi had been worried about how the region would contribute to her local office, had taken a much bigger view of things having taken on a regional coordinator role:

"The merger has brought me new areas of responsibility. For example I manage a particular programme with managers from 15 other countries to do with trust building between communities. For me, getting people to accept me doing that and having a growing sense of confidence made me feel very happy that the change programme had actually happened".

After the Dar meeting Gabriel, a country director from West Africa, found the courage to address long-standing issues of poor performance, giving staff the choice to apply for positions in the new organisation or to move on:

"Some of these issues were about people being set in their ways. A lot of people knew they needed to be resolved. Now we've dealt with it and you're kind of free from that baggage. The most overwhelming thing has been the energy and attitude from the new team, although they did lack experience, the attitude has been a complete 180 degree turn. The atmosphere is different. It's like a different organisation".

One of the country directors had suggested before the meeting that we make a video of the discussions as a way of communicating with the whole of the East and West Africa team. This inspired move captures the energy and positive mood of the leadership team for all to see.

Watching the Dar video and noticing what was unleashed there, I'm enormously satisfied because I know we have delivered what the rest of the team of 500 require of their leadership: courage, decisiveness and integrity; and that there is clarity, confidence and commitment across the organisation to what we can achieve.

■ How do you approach this phase?

In the early phases of the merger, we constantly felt as though we were dragging the group and they were slow to find their own energy. Now, finally, the group seemed not only aligned with one another but also in a trusted position with their people back in country, in other words, ready to lead. We needed them to bring their passion to the life-threatening challenges and find solutions that would move us forward and in doing so, the group needed to become the gazelles of the fable – lean, adaptable and ready to run energetically together to find the best pastures.

Self-organising to motivate people

Harrison Owen, a management "guru" who has organised conferences all over the world from small West African villages to global corporations, has developed a method for larger groups to self-organise in a highly energetic and productive meeting around any issue of shared concern (Owen, 1997). This method called Open Space Technology includes one law, the so-called Law of Two Feet which says: "*if any person finds him or herself in a situation where they are neither learning nor contributing, they must use their two feet and go to some more productive place*". This reminded us we need to give people choice about which topic they work with and the opportunity to express to others their passion for their chosen topic. Once people had chosen to work on a particular topic and given the choice to switch groups, their levels of commitment and motivation increased.

What's the real dilemma?

When confronted with a challenge, it is often easy for a group to gloss over the difficulty of the choices that they face. On the face of it, what is the dilemma in customer service? Do we provide lousy service that generates angry, upset customers or do we provide excellent service that leaves customers surprised and delighted? The answer seems obvious but offers no real sense of why this group had previously been unable to deliver.

Each life threatening issue was difficult to address because it contained buried and paralysing dilemmas, that is choices where both options seemed bad or both options good, for example to close a service outlet is bad because it denies access to customers but to leave it open is also bad because it consumes budget. Charles Hampden-Turner looked at the problem of reconciling dilemmas and showed that when people "work" with a dilemma a third option typically emerges which combines and transcends the other two (Hampden-Turner, 1990). Of the many ways he describes to approach this – mapping, contextualising, sequencing, combining etc – we chose simply to ask participants to present the dilemma as two, mutually exclusive and difficult, options A and B. When the large plenary group gave their feedback on the options, this proved extremely useful in opening up a new way forward for the group as a whole.

To help the team find its position in relation to the dilemmas confronting them, we used an approach called "constellations". This is a method developed by Bert Hellinger, a German family therapist, who found that his methods were also powerful in organisations (Hellinger and Ten Heovel, 1999). It involves people being physically assigned to stand in a position in the room. The position they stand in represents through distance and direction, their relation to other parts of the larger system and from this position they report how they feel and why. This physical method helped us to understand people's views on the dilemmas and for everyone to literally vote with their feet on the direction we might take. It also inspired various activities we used to make the workshop highly dynamic and energetic, including for example the influence circle, line-ups in relation to the dilemmas and a "walking in the dark" exercise to sensitise the group to issues of letting go and trusting others to work on their behalf.

Who are we now?

Richard Pascale, a business school professor, has researched the subject of corporate transformation, studying companies which have succeeded in fundamentally shifting their ways of operating including British Airways, Honda and Ciba (Pascale et al, 1993). He realised that fundamental transformation is not achieved simply through doing. What people do at work arises from an operating "paradigm" or set of assumptions tied in to their identity. A shift in the identity of the company or "who they are being" is needed before a new operating paradigm can be made to stick. When we asked the group of 30 "*Who are you being right now in this workshop, and who are you going to be when you get back to the workplace?*" they answered "*we are the decision-makers*". Asking this question seemed to capture and internalise the positive and energetic spirit of the workshop. It provoked what Francisco Varela called "autopoiesis" or emergent identity (Maturana and Varela, 1988).

Remembering the lack of action after the Nairobi workshop two years earlier, we were very concerned to create conditions for participants to be really mobilised and to be doing things differently after they had finished the Dar Es Salaam meeting. Gerry Johnson is a professor of strategy who has studied strategy workshops comparing them to rituals found in other walks of life (Bourque and Johnson, 2008). He says rituals – including for example, primitive rites of passage, marriages and funerals – involve a separation from everyday life and a kind of performance bringing symbolic communication, strong emotions and the ability to cause transformations. There are three stages: *separation* from old identity, an in-between *liminal* period in which there are images of death and rebirth and then finally, a *reintegration* into society in a new status.

Johnson's research highlights the success of strategy consultants in the first two phases but also shows that consultants are less successful in managing reintegration. A simple action plan does not have sufficient symbolic power. He suggests a series of workshops may be needed and better preparations for the emotional not just the cognitive challenges when participants face the dilemmas of applying the strategy back in the workplace.

As a result, we spent more time tapping into passion as a sustaining energy, surfacing the real dilemmas within the workshop, building trust and consensus in the leadership team, clarifying and signing off actions, rehearsing a single communication message to take back and making explicit the groups' shift in identity. The video was an incredibly powerful tool not just in communicating back to the team of 500 but also as an aide-memoire for the leadership group, reconfirming who they had become through the story played out on film.

Two do-able actions

Harold Sirkin and colleagues at Boston Consulting Group (Sirkin et al, 2005) studied change programmes taking place in 225 companies and discovered a consistent correlation between success or failure around four key factors: Duration, Integrity/capability of the team, Commitment and Effort, making the acronym DICE. Put simply, short duration projects run by capable teams backed by commitment of leaders and staff and requiring little additional effort by staff to implement, these types of projects succeed. Each factor can be simply quantified and an unsurprising but often over-looked key to project success is to arrange things so that staff need to put in no more than 10% extra effort above their day job.

Typically, in the closing stages of a workshop under considerable pressure to commit, people make long lists of actions. A key to our success in Dar and beyond was to ask each group for only two concrete, doable actions that they were confident they could deliver on before the next workshop in 5–6 months.

■ What are the signs of progress?

1. When individuals recognise that if they are neither learning nor contributing, it is their responsibility – not that of the leader – to find a place where they can be productive (Harrison Owen).
2. When the group face up to the really difficult dilemmas and are able to transcend those difficulties to find a way forward (Charles Hampden-Taylor).
3. When individuals in the group recognise how they achieve influence within that group and beyond (Bert Hellinger).
4. When the group is able to recognise a shift in their identity – who they are being – by putting it into words (Richard Pascale).
5. When the group is able to commit to actions, openly owning responsibility for delivering on those and able to describe how that will happen in a realistic way on returning to their workplace (Gerry Johnson).

■ What are the tools you can use?

In this final phase, the five tools which follow give the leader ways to engage others in addressing these key questions: *What is the reality of the big challenges we face? How do we build momentum and confidence in the team?*

No 1: Finding your place in the story

One of the new members of our leadership team told us that arriving in the group was like coming into a cinema when the film was half way through. If they were going to make sense of what was going on next, they needed to understand what had happened in the bit they had missed. Each time we brought the group of 30 together, there were some new faces appearing and some familiar faces missing. To get us moving quickly and purposefully in the meeting, we discovered that to spend 60-90 minutes bringing everyone up to speed with the story to date was very valuable. We introduced the new people, asked them to pair up with existing members and to catch up with the story by reflecting on the experiences and lessons gained in the earlier phases of the story. Insights were posted on wallcharts and played back to the group.

At the end of this, each person knew the others in the group, they had caught up with the plot and the achievements of the whole group had been remembered and celebrated.

This honours a principle called "self-reference" (Wheatley, 1992) whereby a system is strengthened and freed up to change by keeping a memory of its evolutionary path, referring to its past history and identity as a reference point for change. This has proved an enormously powerful tool in building a new team identity.

No 2: The "givens", survival challenges and groups

Philip as leader worked with his immediate colleagues to identify "the givens": these were a set of clear guiding principles that as leader he needed to make plain. For example: as a matter of policy library space will close. These principles helped the entire team to understand the shift and reposition themselves: not simply to rearrange deck chairs on the ship but to construct a completely new ship, going on a very different journey. With the givens stated, it was possible to articulate a small number of life-threatening problems that team members needed to address. We identified six "survival challenges": income, impact, structure, customer excellence, outreach, and brand. Team members were invited to self-organise into six equal-sized groups choosing a challenge to which they were motivated to contribute.

No 3. Dynamic plenaries

The Dar meeting alternated between small group work and plenaries in order to gain whole group input and sign-off for the small group work on the survival challenges. This alternation could have become boring had we not challenged each small group to be highly engaging and creative in maintaining the energy of the meeting. Quickly they learned that debate in plenary is draining, so a practice evolved where after their presentation, a small group would invite questions, but instead of batting back answers they would simply note the questions and take them away as feedback. Other devices included "everyone stand up until you support the direction proposed then sit down"; "skits" on customer service; a "market place" for selling solutions; "gallery walks" to share information; "speed-dating" to make deals with colleagues; and two minute "elevator pitches" for a punchy persuasive sell.

No 4. What is our identity? Who are we now?

We realised that at Dar the group had been working together in a very different way as leaders of the region. This shift was evident to us but we were not sure if it was evident to everyone in the team or whether it would be easy to sustain when they got back home. We asked the group to answer a couple of questions: *Who are we being here in Dar? Who will you be when you get back to your countries?* Their answers served to confirm to all that they had taken on a new identity here. They had become leaders taking decisions on behalf of the region. Team members decided that they wanted to continue holding on to this identity on their return to their country operations.

No 5. Bringing it back home – the video

Back in the country operations, people were waiting for the leaders stepping off the plane to find out what had been decided: *Do I still have a job? What is going to happen now? What did you talk about?* But it is difficult for anyone to convey all the insights, messages, decisions and above all, the spirit of the meeting. At the Dar meeting, one of the Country Directors decided to make a video, catching key parts of the discussion, interviewing participants and showing the range of issues discussed. At the end of this, he produced a ten minute video including reports from all six challenge groups. A copy was provided to each country.

■ What is the evidence of completing this phase?

- The group stops prevaricating and dancing around and finally grips the issues in their entirety.
- The group is able to organise themselves into work teams and to make and take forward decisions on behalf of and accountable to the leadership community deciding new ways of working appropriate to the new situation.
- There is a shared sense of momentum, confidence and inspiration – a pride in who the group are and what they are achieving.
- The group is able to define its identity as a leadership team and to communicate that to the wider team for which it is responsible.
- The burden of decision-making shifts from the leader to the leadership community as a whole.

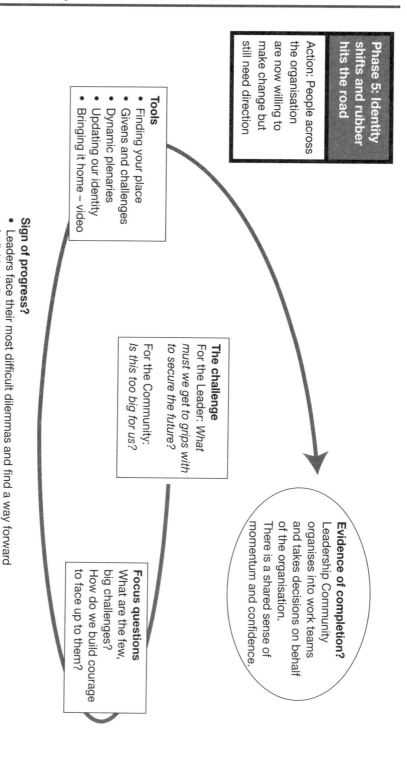

Phase 5: Identity shifts and rubber hits the road

Action: People across the organisation are now willing to make change but still need direction

Tools
- Finding your place
- Givens and challenges
- Dynamic plenaries
- Updating our identity
- Bringing it home – video

The challenge
For the Leader: *What must we get to grips with to secure the future?*

For the Community: *Is this too big for us?*

Evidence of completion?
Leadership Community organises into work teams and takes decisions on behalf of the organisation. There is a shared sense of momentum and confidence.

Focus questions
What are the few, big challenges? How do we build courage to face up to them?

Sign of progress?
- Leaders face their most difficult dilemmas and find a way forward
- Individuals find a place where they can be productive
- Leaders commit to action, knowing how to engage others in the wider team to deliver

Tips

- A short video is a fantastic communication tool particularly in conveying the personality of a meeting but make sure you have a storyboard before you start filming. If not, you are going to have hours and hours of editing ahead of you.
- Congratulations! You've built a strong sense of team but make sure new members joining your group are not overwhelmed by the robust identity of your group. Pay attention to how new team members are integrated and welcomed if they are going to get up to speed quickly and feel included.
- Support and mentor the work groups once they are back in the workplace. Stay in touch. Encourage them to keep in touch with each other. Recognise what they are doing and help those who encounter obstacles to overcome them.
- However much progress you make, the job is never completely done. Realistically there is always the risk that issues and habits you have tackled creep back into the team's way of working because of lack of attention, forgetfulness or laziness. Don't be disappointed, but don't ignore this – be deliberate about reminding people and keeping them alert to their promises.

Part 3

The Path

The path to alignment

As we come to the end of this story, we face a key question: why did this change programme deliver when so few do? We know our success in aligning the team has helped to ensure the delivery of ever improving, business results, but how do we demonstrate this?

Imagine you are a coal-miner whose pit has closed "for economic and political reasons": might you not feel sadness or anger at the fate that has befallen you? So it would be for a trainer standing in the empty shell that remains after their poorly performing teaching centre is shut, or any other employee in this organisation. When change has been imposed from on high, you create losers not leaders.

Prior experience had taught us that while it is uncomfortable to close offices and sack people, it is not difficult to reduce costs by imposing cuts like this. What is much more difficult is to mobilise people to step up to face their own challenges, causing them to respond creatively and take tough but innovative decisions themselves, thus to be leaders not losers.

As our change programme gathered pace, we found that when we brought teams together from across the region, this created a growing awareness of the challenge they shared and disseminated new ways of delivering results. Whatever worked was quickly copied. Akello describes how her country built on another's success in delivering a new regional product.

"One of the countries started off in a really interesting way. They had gone to the radio and TV stations and succeeded in getting thousands of young people excited and talking about development goals to the whole country. It was very inspiring and I talked with my colleagues there to find out how they managed to reach such large numbers. We then took up the same initiative in our country. It was very easy because we weren't reinventing the wheel. We also learnt from another country about getting through to the youth ministry and getting access on the ground and we copied that too".

Somehow the set of conditions we had created sparked off a "can-do" attitude and a solution-led culture that spread quickly from the 30 leaders through all 500 staff and out into all the key relationships. Mark, one of the senior and most experienced country directors, is in no doubt about the results and the benefits of this approach:

"It benefits all our target audiences – and as employees we have more belief in ourselves. Our customers understand what we're doing and why we're doing it. We have a newer and simpler narrative which is about "creating opportunities for young people and modernising UK-African relationships". It's easier to communicate and more satisfying to do … although there's still a hell of a long way to go".

Typically change comes to a rapid halt when a restructuring threatens people's jobs, but during this two year period more than half the people in this region faced such a situation. Gail, newly promoted to country director and arriving in a new country with a poor performing office, tapped into the experience of a colleague in another country to address this situation:

"We started having gentle but honest conversations with staff about why we were continuing to do stuff we've been doing for years, communicating the region's strategy early on, including evidence of what we're good at and what we need to work on. We got teams working on the gaps, so by the time I announced the structure none of it was news to them! We let people choose openly between voluntary redundancy or applying for jobs in the new structure alongside external applicants. Quite a few we wanted to retain opted to go and do something else, and obviously we had people who wanted to stay and didn't get jobs but I think their transition was well managed too. We even held a party to celebrate the success we'd had in the past and to mark the end of an era. Some people who were leaving said 'thank you' to me. We now have a team in place who are able to deliver".

Rarely do we hear of restructuring addressed with such dignity all round.

While most change initiatives quickly run out of steam, the East and West Africa team has gone forward since the Dar meeting, finding it easier and easier to identify and solve new challenges. The leadership community has become accustomed to tackling difficult dilemmas, taking concrete actions, keeping their teams on-board. They work successfully with conflict and difference both in the group and outside it. All in all, they have become something quite special. Moreover, we have not experienced change fatigue.

Foluke, one of our African senior manager describes it like this:

> "*Changes come and go and often an organisation reverts to established behaviour patterns. This change program took it to the next level …. This was change which has made a difference.*"

Delivering the business results throughout this period has been essential but it is the continuing strength of the team in meeting each new challenge that, for us, is the more remarkable part of the story. We have analysed and set out the key steps that created the "can do" ethos in this team and described it as a "path to alignment" that we think will help others facing similar challenges. Here it is in summary (see overleaf).

Now, let us see what this tells us about the role of the leader. On the *Titanic* the Captain presumed to know more than those in the engine room, with a disastrous result. When we are dealing with complex, large scale change, not only do we need to overturn the notion that the leader is the one with all the answers, but also a second notion that the leader is the only one with the right questions! In fact, we believe the whole point of engagement is that it is a two way process. The leader needs to find out and respond to unasked questions from others at each stage, and unless this happens progress falters. The leader has to continue even though the unasked and unanswered questions can at first, be quite negative such as: *How can I get through this without changing? What is the leader being so stupid and nasty?*

Looking back at the Path to Alignment and the Fable, some simple but fundamental principles are apparent:

1. There is a **pattern** that you should be aware of – the fable is a short metaphoric description of it, and the five phases of our story are a specific example of how people align around any organisational or social change – from a small office reshuffle to a Russian perestroika, to dealing with global climate change.
2. It is **two way** – first an individual engages a community of leaders through talking **and** listening. Then, they go out as individual leaders to engage other individuals and groups in the wider organisation or society.
3. **Leaders transmit and multiply** – success depends on having leaders who know how to enlist leaders from those who are initially reluctant bystanders or suffering victims, as well as from those who are enthusiastic "early adopters". Leaders work not only to transmit but to multiply energies,

The path to alignment across an organisation

Phase and action	The challenge	Focus questions	Signs of progress	Tools	Evidence of completion
1. Looming danger and making the first call. The leader alerts the leadership community.	For the Leader: *How do I deliver this message?* For the Community: *How can I get through this without changing?*	Where are we now? What does the future look like? What are the first steps?	• The leader is motivating not frightening people • The challenge is clearly and explicitly framed	• 6 Thinking Hats • Visioning 5/1/3 • Transition Planning • 5 Min Process Review	• Leadership Community united in inaction, trying to maintain the status quo. • Leader thwarted or tricked into believing others are engaged.
2. Lame response and making the second call. The call is ignored, the leader pushes harder.	For the Leader: *How do I wake them up?* For the Community: *Why is the leader being so stupid and nasty?*	What's new? How do we recover control? What do we keep/let go of?	• People are exposed to new attitudes and behaviours • Resistance is recognised and explored • 75% know change is necessary	• Stakeholder Contact • Three Circles • The Mirror • Timeline	• Leadership Community step from the past into the future, but may feel sad and lost. • Leader may be angry, at the group's resistance.
3. Leadership Community aligns and steps up. The community falls apart then regroups.	For the Leader: *How do I transfer ownership?* For the Community: *How can I influence?*	What do I know? What do you know? How do we take decisions?	• People grapple with how to change • Members unite • Individuals find an action they are passionate to implement.	• Thing of Beauty • Steering Group • Social Mapping and Swarms	• Leadership Community are bonded, engaged and confident. "We know what we need to do". • Leader feels relief and progress.
4. People pull back … then embrace the new reality. The leadership community takes the change back home.	For the Leader: *How do we engage the wider team?* For the Community: *Now I'm enthusiastic why is my team not?*	What do you want from me? What do I want from you?	• Staff share both +/– stories • Difficult issues are on the table • Leaders commit to simple actions and behaviours	• Staff Research • Stories – Talking in the Round • Action Plans	• Staff speak up on issues that concern them. • Leadership Community recognise how their behaviour contributes. • All "in the same boat".
5. Identity shifts and rubber hits the road People are willing to make change but still need direction.	For the Leader: *What must get to grips with?* For the Community: *Is this too big for us?*	What are the few, big challenges? How do we build courage to face up to them?	• Leaders face dilemmas and commit to action • Individuals find ways to be productive	• Finding Your Place • Givens & Challenges • Dynamic Plenaries • Updating Our Identity • Bringing It Home – Video	• Leadership Community organises on behalf of the organisation. • Shared sense of momentum.

build capacity and transform identities in order to deliver performance and change.

4. **Leaders transform themselves** – in each phase of the process the initiating leader adopts a slightly different role stepping backwards, forwards or sideways to provide the best balance of context, challenge and support, releasing and channelling the energies of others, constantly doing what is needed to re-inject life and focus to the process.

5. **This is magic** – not in the sense of hocus-pocus but because the effect is at certain moments, dramatic, unexpected and positive.

As these principles became apparent during the Africa merger, we were able to observe the dynamics in a totally different way: the process of alignment became a dialogue, like a dance with a rhythm, like the "to and fro" or "call and response" that you find for example in African drumming. You gain control over the pace, not by speaking faster or pushing on with the action, but by slowing down, listening and responding more directly to the people that need to be engaged. The leadership "guru", Warren Bennis observes it like this:

> "In a day gone by, running an organisation seemed akin to conducting a symphony orchestra. Nowadays, I think it's more like leading a jazz ensemble. There's more improvisation. Someone once wrote that the sound of surprise is jazz, and if there is anything we need to cultivate a taste for in this world, it is surprise, the unexpected, the unimaginable. In essence, we need to acquire a taste for change" (Bennis, 2000, p vii).

In Africa, we discovered that while the moment might be a long time coming, alignment actually occurs in an instant of magic when something in the mind of the team goes "click" and simultaneously, a group realises its new identity. And for us, this happened in phase three in Addis and again in phase five in Dar Es Salaam. We believe that the team wants to form this identity – that they do have what we call an "urge to merge".

How was this achieved? We had been inspired by Francisco Varela (Maturana and Varela, 1988) to think of the merged East and West Africa Region as an "organism", or "eco-system" and to create the new identity or boundary by asking the individual members: *"Who are you being collectively right now? What is your shared interest? What is your collective role?"*. At the beginning these questions would only have yielded negative remarks along the lines of *"we are being hippos and we have no pooled interest"*. Through the groundwork, over a period of two years we created the conditions for those instances of magic to take place. How?

Instead of packing the agenda with ad-hoc urgent topics, we created at the start of each group of 30 meeting a "context for action" by exploring with the group their story of the "organism", including its history, present health, future opportunities and dangers. The meeting was never an isolated event unconnected to the work outside the confines of the meeting room. It was part of a story that connected to previous meetings and all that we had accomplished (or not) in between. This placed everyone – whether they were new or old in this team – in a tradition of performance. They owned that performance – good or bad – collectively from the moment they stepped into the team. Instead of behaving as victims having change imposed on them, the team began to operate as active players in the story, in charge of determining the next chapter. This re-made them into leaders who are purposeful and aligned like gazelles.

When you stop to think about alignment it has an inner and outer aspect. Inner alignment is when our heads, hearts and hands are aligned; the process is personal change and the positive effect is that our energy is fully available to us. Outer alignment occurs between people in partnerships and teams; the process is the call and response of dialogue and the positive effect is we can combine our energies and multiply our impact. The work of aligning a team keeps coming back to where they are right now, and advancing from there in doable, motivated steps. We have shown how transformation is possible when such small steps are sustained. We have looked for ways to speed this up but we have realised it requires time, dedication and a constancy of commitment from the leadership.

Our approach replaces some outdated paternalistic ideas about leadership particularly the idea of the "knight in the white charger" or the "controlling parent to dependent child" or the "charismatic leader directing their congregation". In our experience, these contribute little to the success of a merger or change programme and cause a lot of misery both to leader and led. As an alternative, we are describing a "leader who creates leaders". This is not a simple giving away of power but a shift in identity by the leader from which flows a deliberate and careful process of engaging individuals to expand their contribution.

We have learned that in order to transform people into a high performing team, senior managers have first to transform themselves. As Gabriel, a country director, describes it:

"The thing that we're talking about here is not just change-about-them, but it's a change-about-us".

This is a story about Philip learning that, to influence one has to be influenced, and changing his mindset to "one head does not contain all the wisdom". This has meant adjusting his approach from simply pushing hard in the first two phases to a much more nuanced approach in which the emotional journey of the group is recognised and embraced by the leader. Philip realised that instead of trying to simply command and dominate, he needed to step in and out with care and intelligence, one moment asking for help, then at another time giving a steer, helping the group to move itself forward.

Meanwhile Tony has been learning about the galvanising effect of courage. He has been surprised that in this project, his most exciting facilitation for many years, he has become engaged ever more deeply in the challenge of engaging others. Particularly in Lagos and Dar, Tony noticed himself going beyond the ordinary, taking bigger risks, making confident moves out of difficulty, believing more and more in what he was doing and achieving ever greater impact. This stemmed in part from the confidence the group of 30 were investing in him, partly from the ballsy "let's do it" attitude of Philip, and partly because Ben was frequently reminding him to simply laugh spontaneously, trust himself and enjoy just doing it without over-analysing.

From this Tony gained a renewed sense of himself and his particular brand of facilitation and coaching. He realised his "real work" is to bring others into their power, make their eyes sparkle, and to pursue the ripple effect, creating conditions which multiply engagement across an entire organisation. This involves moving leaders backward or forward – depending on their habit either out of passivity or out of dominance – into or out of the firelight, finding a way to take charge so that others around them step up too.

Working together we have shown how a facilitator and a leader can transform behaviour, mobilising a group and an entire organisation. We have done this not as a brief one-off that quickly runs out of steam, but as a sustainable way of delivering top performance. Together the facilitator and leader influence in hundreds of small (and large) ways how each person experiences themselves, their colleagues and the group. With a new "take" on the situation, each person not only begins to behave differently, but can redefine who they are. There are many examples of this happening. For example:

- **Fatima** who made a stand for local staff being heard in the very first meeting, who had her eyes opened as a result and changed her vision of how to work in the organisation.
- Remember **Binte,** shocked when first asked to attend the workshop but who later on was asking herself "*is this really me standing in front of colleagues providing them with knowledge*".
- **Ian** who shrugged his shoulders at first but then made the brave early moves in a small influential group which set things in motion.
- **Yahya** who earlier was adamant that in Africa pecking order and strong hierarchical leadership are important, later recognised how a leader must also be supportive, making people creative and carrying everyone along.
- **Akello** who at first was unable to see how a big region could benefit her small provincial office, then later felt empowered to take on a regional responsibility bringing people from 15 other countries to a major project she was coordinating.
- **Otim** unsure of what to make of regionalisation, first took on a role of communicating changes to staff and then became a confident team leader of country directors charged with finding new sources of income.
- **Foluke** who at first appeared quiet and shy, then found her voice in giving clear and objective feedback to the leadership team on some highly contentious staff issues which in turn, propelled a deeper shift in their attitudes and behaviour.
- For **Gail**, frustrated and unable to get heard or understood in a leadership team dominated by men, the gender issue completely went away. She fundamentally transformed her country office from dark, dingy and down in the dumps to one that delivers and is now at the forefront of regional innovation.
- **Gabriel** coming in half way through "the film" caught the change bug and feeling enthused and energised set off to tackle some long standing performance issues, liberating his office from the shackles of the past and creating an overwhelmingly positive "can-do" attitude amongst his team.
- **Mark** who admits to initial cynicism based on some difficult previous experiences of regionalisation became a convert, recognised for his creative talent and becoming a leading light in taking the organisation's new agenda forward.

This story has shown how 30 leaders make a difference to the performance of 500 staff spread across a wide geographical area. The personal transformation in each leader creates new behaviour and performance in the staff that surround them. This effect has been amplified and consolidated in a few critical ways including communication:

> *"Philip sends a monthly newsletter and there are bulletins to all staff so you know what is expected and nothing comes as a surprise. It tells people what has been going on, what we are still doing, what has been going well, what the challenges are, how we need to improve ourselves… so that kind of keeps you on your toes of what is really happening".*

… harmonised terms and conditions, through a single regional pay and grade structure:

> *"The terms and conditions have varied but now we have new terms and conditions which staff appreciate very much. This helped us to no longer say "my country is different, the East is different form the West". A lot of issues have been synchronised and that has helped with staff morale".*

… a recognition scheme:

> *"They introduced a scheme, really looking through at what people do and giving you the chance to nominate yourself, a colleague or a group that you think have performed particularly well, especially in the drive towards our strategic plan. This comes with a financial reward, not big but big enough to tell you you've been recognised for it. Then on top of that, there is the noticing and the naming – it is copied to everyone in the region, so everyone knows. Because this has come out, it encourages people to do things and to notice when they feel their colleagues are doing their best. It makes people feel proud and also to feel I need to get my act together".*

….and a comprehensive training programme with self-study modules supported by trained coaches.

As Binte illustrates, the effect has been felt by people throughout the organisation:

> *"A colleague who has been in the library for years finds out the library is closing. He is afraid of losing his job and he is afraid that he doesn't have the capacity to deliver the new products because he felt it is moving him from what he knows and exposes him to a wider context that he doesn't know. He was asking himself "do I have the skills to meet the challenge?" Now, he has taken on the role of Project Manager for the pan-African schools project and it was*

like a promotion in the sense that he is coordinating a regional programme, linking with colleagues in other countries. It's boosted his capacity!"

The sum effect of all this change is 500 individuals aligning by letting go of the past, regrouping, stepping up to a new challenge and moving into a new chapter. Their shared organisational story was first articulated by the leadership team in Dar:

"When we started two years ago, we were East and West, separate countries, separate regions, possessive, parochial, suspicious and not wanting to share. The region was all hot air and nothing real.

There were lots of things needing to be challenged and done in order to create a sustainable platform from which to develop regional products that customers valued and staff believed in.

Each of our leadership meetings raised difficult questions, created challenging situations and uncovered precious moments which helped bring us through to where we are now. In particular, Lagos taught us about leadership, leadership, leadership and how despite the tension that comes from change you can still engage and energise everyone, despite all the difficulties of geography and numbers.

Now, as decision-makers for the region we are creating success, reputation and enjoyment. We are not afraid of challenges or diversity".

So whilst the improvement in business results as a result of this change is something we feel very proud of, the positive change in individuals, and in the team as a whole, is an amazing tribute to the ability of people to transform themselves when they have the right conditions.

The bigger relevance of these conclusions is economic and social. For example, Douglass C North (2005), a Nobel prize winning economist, has demonstrated how "institutional rigidity" is the biggest barrier to economic progress in all countries but notably in the poorest places on earth such as Cameroon where year after year things fail to improve. By "institution" North means the unwritten rules, assumptions, beliefs and behaviours which determine results. One of the greatest mysteries of change is why so much technical expertise, money and other resources are put into it for so little result. The "path to alignment" is the most powerful way we know to break down rigidities, erode the cycle of poor performance and dependency and to create results through and alongside, sustainable change across an entire organisation.

Philip's organisation, British Council, was originally established 75 years ago to project the public face of British culture to the world and this was perceived to be of national interest. Today, its role has changed dramatically to be multi-faceted, seeking to break down barriers to understanding and build long-term, trust-based and mutually-beneficial relationships (Fiske, 2007). This approach to cultural relations contributes directly to tackling serious global issues such as climate change, conflict and misunderstanding between communities and societies, as well as strengthening the international profile and engagement of the UK in the arts, English and education. Making this new strategic agenda real for the 500 staff in East and West Africa and the 7500 staff working for British Council globally, has been no small challenge. It has been a test that British Council senior executives have been grappling with in all corners of the globe. Their success can be seen in the shift to a much more focused strategy and programme, the introduction of new partnerships and programmes and an exponential increase in their audience, reaching many millions more through their work in only a matter of years.

During the merger and change programme, Philip's approach as a leader has used the British Council's cultural relations expertise to great effect in delivering internal change. This has meant leading in a particular way: based on the mutuality principle, influencing through seeking to be influenced, listening, call and response. The region's improved performance and its increased capacity to adapt, have taken a big leap forward through a kind of leadership which aligns everyone, while turning each person into a leader and a walking, talking example of cultural relations.

9 If you do this, you will be on the right track …

Our story is a magical one about how leadership can transform – turning hippos into gazelles. It is a story about the power of numbers where one leader can engage 30 who in turn, engage 500 others to create an organisation that is aligned in its purpose and that is suddenly willing and able to deliver.

This approach works. In the two years covered by our story, the East & West Africa region was able to transform its business with:

- A threefold increase in its customer base
- An 80% increase in its income across its three major business areas
- A 10% reduction in its cost base
- Leadership results that match top ten performing companies in the UK (covering both public and private sector). This included results for "leadership of change" that are twice as positive as the top ten companies.

This overall result translates positively into a liberation and new momentum for 11 country operations and almost 500 staff. In Gail's words:

"There's a story to be told of an office being run on very hierarchical lines with a very unclear programme seen as a sort of donor agency because that was the interest of the people working here. It is a journey the team has taken from stopping all of that and getting into being much more outward focused with some very dynamic staff, all of whom are locally appointed. We listen to our customers, have more fun and are much more creative and involved. Our voice is now being heard in the region. We've got a big old colonial building that before was small rooms, dark and dingy and now we've opened up the space, got great colours everywhere and it's a different place! Now we're seen as a country which delivers!"

One year on from where our story ends, the region's results have been sustained and improved, and as we come to the end of our book, what are the headlines we want to leave you with? What would we share with leaders who are about to embark on their own journey of merger or change?

Clearly any leader's job is to influence the behaviour and performance of others. But how? Here are ten pointers to put you on the right track.

1. The leader has a clear message but does not have all the answers

… nor do they have all the right questions! In an age when managers are bombarded with information, the leader makes a difference because their message helps focus their people on the few important things they need to pay attention to, for the benefit of all. The effective leader sets the environment in which the right questions, answers and solutions emerge and in which purposeful action can be taken to deliver those solutions.

As you take on a leadership role, you'll feel the temptation to show your team just exactly what it is you know and why you have been appointed. There is the lure to push them hard with your action plans to revolutionise the organisation. The risk is that the team will simply dig their heels in, they refuse to contribute; they roar and they bite and before long you are caught up, just another hippo fighting in the mud! Remember the African proverb *"one head does not contain all the wisdom"*.

2. Actions speak volumes

Leaders reinforce their message through their stories, their decisions and their behaviour and this sends people much stronger signals than just telling them what to do. When leaders say one thing and do another, feelings of cynicism grow exponentially. When leaders say one thing and do nothing, a pervading sense of powerlessness infects the organisation. Simple, highly visible changes that reinforce your message, will make lights flash, bells ring, whistles blow!

Reminding your team what you said you would do and regularly updating them on progress, reinforces a sense of purpose and momentum. It is amazing how energising it is for your team to see through concrete actions, that you mean what you say, that you walk the talk. And when it doesn't go so well, it is better to share this with your team. They will trust you more and it will add to the credibility of your success stories. Courtesy, warmth, a simple "hello", asking for someone's opinion – quite small behaviours make a world of difference in winning hearts and minds.

3. The leader steps back

The leader is rightly focused on results but tends to push too fast in trying to achieve them. When they do this the team is knocked off balance and they close up or block. When the young chief shook his stick, the other chiefs resisted him by getting angry or falling asleep. A leader behaving like this stops the team from stepping up. The leader who simply toughens up will just push the team into a corner.

If instead, you can soften, step back and listen, you create space for the team. This allows people to become more engaged, to step up to the plate themselves and create new possibilities. Good facilitation helps this process: get all the help you can!

4. Good leadership is like the sound of jazz

All leaders ask for something from their teams – they make the call. Good leaders hear the reply and ponder. High performance leaders constantly engage with their teams, consciously building up an interplay between leader and led. When done with care and purpose, this becomes a dialogue like the call and return of a jazz improvisation – sometimes surprising, sometimes beautiful, sometimes unnerving – but building resolutely and with understanding over time, on each note that has come before.

As a leader, you gain control over this, not by simply speaking louder, moving faster or pushing on with the action, but by slowing down, listening and responding more directly to exactly what you are hearing. Listen carefully to others, and listen to yourself.

5. You need the head, the hands and the heart

A leader is effective only when they balance the three agendas of logic, implementation and emotion, in other words thinking, doing and feeling. The young chief used his head to warn the other chiefs of the danger they faced. He used his hands to wave his stick when they wouldn't listen to him. He used his heart when he saw their fear and concern and responded by changing his behaviour and asking them to sit with him. This sent the powerful message to others that he needed their help, that no one (not even the leader) could do this on their own.

Different behaviour is needed from you at different stages of the change process – from creating an intellectual argument for change, to engaging with and listening to people, to creating the space for people to step up and lead. You need to be a flexible chief and consider what is required in each moment.

The beneficial impact of this kind of leadership on the team is commitment, motivation, positive energy, and you start to lay the foundations for a new team identity. Like the head, heart and hands of a healthy human being working in harmony, if your people are engaged by the What, the Why and the How you can deliver a healthy and successful merger or change programme.

6. The leader sets their teams to work

Implementing change across large, dispersed organisations means it is impossible for all senior managers to be involved in every decision. Trying to do this means that decisions simply don't get made. Everyone gets stuck in a traffic jam of choices waiting for a green light that never comes. Colleagues need to be trusted to work on behalf of a team which in turn is working on behalf of the organisation. To repay and further build this trust they need to make themselves accountable to the organisation.

Getting senior managers – including you – to let go of authority requires a high degree of trust across the organisation. This requires you to spend time together defining the biggest issues that need to be addressed, agreeing approaches to those problems and assigning teams to take them forward. The initial alignment takes time and effort but once you have a sign-off for each team's approach, let them get on with it!

7. Doing is inspiring

Simply talking about change makes people feel uncertain, insecure and fearful. What will the new world be like? Where do I fit in? Do I have a part to play? Many organisations make the mistake of making change difficult, spending months and years navel-gazing, only to find that, when they are finally ready to implement a change, the outside world has packed its bags, moved on and left them behind.

You need to begin from where your people are, make doable steps, show them immediately the impact they achieved by acting together, and celebrate success early, to create the confidence to push on quickly. Then change starts to be fun! Good leaders make it simple and practical, allowing their people quickly to move into new ways of working and to experience the benefits that change makes to their customers. Don't get lost like so many have in the maze of change!

8. The leader creates new identities

People desire identity, purpose and meaning in their life: if you ignore this, your only route to change is force and your results will be short-lived. At work, a person's survival, territory, habits and relationships with colleagues all contribute to their sense of identity, and it's no surprise that people resist the break-up of what defines them, whether they like the current circumstances or not. Recognising this, the leader needs to create special situations where people can open themselves up to the possibility of change and later to create a new sense of identity and belonging.

The leader is like a boatman or woman carrying people safely over choppy waters from one side of the river to another. Such a journey is a metaphor for a shift in identity, a transformation in how a person thinks of themself and where they belong.

You do not create a new team identity simply by telling your own story, nor by giving the example of someone else's story. Instead, you enable the team to express their own story. Key to this are three simple questions: *Who were you being then? What happened on the way? Who are you being now?* Although shaky at first, with your help people can quickly become secure, with growing self-esteem and confidence in their new identity. This is called building resilience, and for secure, resilient people, the next change is always easier.

9. The leader is in for the long-haul

Transformation is magic but there's no simple spell. Our story covered two years and there were no short-cuts. Sustainable improvements don't come easy. One participant said you have to be a "positive kind of slave driver". You may be up against a culture of silence, or long-standing issues not dealt with from which you must not back down. You may need to face people with hard choices over whether to stay or exit.

Your positive energy is key to this. It is a long-term commitment and there will be tests of your nerve and ingenuity along the way. Many business leaders talk about getting "buy-in" to change but quickly find their attention wandering. Real change doesn't come without a deep personal commitment from those in charge to working <u>with</u> their people in identifying what is required to build future successes. The deep connection between leaders and their teams necessary to make change happen won't materialise just through the occasional "consultation". It takes emotional intelligence, bravery and hard work from the leadership community to follow up on that commitment.

10. The leader transforms people from victims into leaders of change

For most people change is imposed from outside, a wind of change blowing through the organisation over which they have no control. Inevitably, they begin the change process as victims, nervous about what will happen to them. Whether they continue to feel that way ultimately depends on the role you play as leader, and your willingness to take into account the nine principles above. You have the authority and the opportunity to turn people from passive sufferers into enthusiastic and confident leaders of change. It's worth stopping – taking one or two breaths – and recognising the weight of the responsibility you hold and thinking through how you might respond.

Gabriel, one of our country directors, paints a vivid picture of what it is like to be the leader:

> *"You go to a typical African market and you've got thousands of sellers, everyone shouting at you to buy this and that. You've got to be very clear about where you're going, and very, very sympathetic but not thrown off track. If you're not clear what you want to listen to and what you want to buy, you end up not actually buying anything. I think that epitomises any change programme. If you're the leader, you've got to be very clear as to what you want to buy, look out for it, and make it through the noise of the market".*

So, these are our signposts. Merger and change is not easy and we cannot pretend otherwise. This is real life and so it will inevitably be a story of ups and downs, of challenges and failures. Nevertheless, leadership provides the opportunity to work some special magic – to transform and improve the lot of your organisation and the people who work in it. Like in any fable, it requires someone with an honest heart and good intent to make that magic work. Great leaders create leaders and in doing so, bring sustainable, long-term results for the organisation. Let us know how you get on.

The End

Bibliography

Bennis, Warren (2000) *Intelligent Leadership – Creating a Passion for Change*. Random House Business Books, p. vii.

Bieshaar, Hans, Knight, Jeremy & van Wassenaer, Alexander (2001) Deals that create value, *McKinsey Quarterly*, February.

Bohm, David (1990) *On Dialogue*. Pegasus.

Bourque, Nicole & Johnson, Gerry (2008) Strategy workshops and 'awaydays' as ritual. Chapter 29 in: G. Hodgkinson & W. Starbuck, *The Oxford Handbook of Organizational Decision Making*. Oxford University Press

Bowlby, John (1951) *Child Care and the Growth of Love*. Harmondsworth: Penguin.

Bresnitz, Shlomo (1989) *Enhancing Performance Under Stress by Information About Its Expected Duration*. Final Report. NTIS.

Bridges, William (1980) *Transitions – Making Sense of Life's Changes*. Nicholas Brealey.

Cooperrider, David & Whitney, Diane (2005) *Appreciative Inquiry – A Positive Revolution in Change*. Berrett-Koehler.

Covey, Stephen (1989) *The Seven Habits of Highly Effective People*. Simon and Schuster.

De Bono, Edward (2000) *Six Thinking Hats*. Penguin.

Denning, Stephen (2004) Telling tales, *Harvard Business Review*. Reprint.

Festinger, Leon (1957) *A Theory of Cognitive Dissonance*. Stanford, CA: Stanford University.

Fiske, Philip (2007) *Learning to Listen*. British Council. (A policy paper on Intercultural dialogue.)

Goleman, Daniel (2003) *Destructive Emotions*. Bloomsbury, p 306.

Greaves, Nick (1988) *When Hippo Was Hairy*. Bok Books.

Hampden-Turner, Charles (1990) *Charting the Corporate Mind – From Dilemma to Strategy*. Wiley Blackwell.

Handy, Charles (2008) *Myself and Other More Important Matters*. Amacom.

Hellinger, Bert & Ten Heovel, Gabriele (1999) *Acknowledging What Is: Conversations With Bert Hellinger*. Zeig, Tucker & Co.

Hirschhorn, Larry (1999) The primary risk, *Human Relations*, 52(1).

Isaacs, William (1999) *Dialogue and the Art of Thinking Together*. Currency.

Kotter, John P. (1995) Leading change – why transformation efforts fail, *Harvard Business Review*, March–April.

Kotter, John & Cohen, Dan (2002) *The Heart of Change*. Harvard Business School.

Kubler-Ross, Elizabeth (1973) *On Death and Dying*. Routledge.

Lewin, Kurt (1997) *Resolving Social Conflicts and Field Theory in Social Science*. American Psychological Association.

Losada, M. & Heaphy, E. (2004) The role of positivity and connectivity in the performance of business teams: a nonlinear dynamics model, *American Behavioral Scientist*, 47(6), pp. 740–765.

Marlier, Didier & Parker, Chris (2008) Engagement leadership – the three agendas of leaders. Manuscript in production.

Maturana, Humberto & Varela, Francisco (1988) *The Tree of Knowledge – The Biological Roots of Human Understanding*. Shambhala.

Mindell, Arnold (1992) *The Leader as Martial Artist*. Harper.

North, Douglass C. (2005) *Understanding the Process of Economic Change*. Princeton.

Oshry, Ben (1996) *Seeing Systems – Unlocking the Mysteries of Organisational Life*. Berrett-Koehler.

Owen, Harrison (1997) *Open Space Technology – A User's Guide*. Berrett-Koehler.

Page, Tony (1996) *Diary of a Change Agent*. Gower.

Page, Tony (2008) Writing stories to facilitate an African merger, *Organisations & People*, 15(1), February.

Pascale, R., Goss, T. & Athos, A. (1993) The reinvention roller coaster – risking the present for a powerful future, *Harvard Business Review*, Nov–Dec.

Prochaska, Janice, Levesque, Deborah & Prochaska, James (2001) Mastering change – a core competency for employees, *Brief Treatment and Crisis Intervention*, 1, Oxford University Press, pp. 7–15.

Schutz, William (1994) *The Human Element – Productivity, Self-esteem and the Bottom Line*. Jossey Bass.

Sirkin, Harold, Keenan, Perry & Jackson, Alan (2005) The hard side of change management, *Harvard Business Review*.

Torbert, Bill (2004) *Action Inquiry – The Secret of Timely and Transforming Leadership*. Berrett-Koehler.

Weisbord, Marvin R. & Janoff, Sandra (1995) *Future Search – An Action Guide to Finding Common Ground in Organisations and Communities*. Berrett-Koehler.

Wheatley, Margaret (1994) *Leadership and the New Science*. Berrett-Koehler.

Acknowledgements

Where does an idea come from? And when you have an idea which conversations and which people originally caused it to crystallise? Who helped this idea to be born as a real ambition, then a plan and eventually the physical paper and print you are holding as you read this? Who encouraged us and helped to keep us motivated along the way?

The answer to all these questions is it is hard to tell, but we do remember and wish to acknowledge several people who made quite memorable contributions:

- Above all the leadership team and staff (both past and present) in British Council's East and West Africa Region. It has been an inspiration to work with them. We hope we have done justice to their dedication, creativity and passion.
- The people from that team who kindly agreed to be interviewed for the book.
- Andy Phillips and Peter Masaaba who did so much of the research with staff that made the breakthrough in Lagos possible.
- Ben Parker who brought his special clarity and big energy on the journey with us from Nairobi to Dar-Es-Salaam (with several other stops on the way).
- Barry Curnow and the Brainstrust participants at CASS Business School in London, to whom, one Tuesday evening in October 2007, we first presented our Tales from Africa.
- Anand Kumar who invited us to write the book and has fired us with ideas and encouragement during its writing.
- John Worne and Nick Wadham-Smith at British Council who saw the value of the idea and have encouraged us to share it.
- The British Council Counterpoint team who have supported us as co-publishers.

- Wendy Mitchell and RDSi the qualitative market research company in London who conducted the field interviews.
- Wilson Page who designed the cover from his student house in Leeds.
- Harriet Stanes who reworked her fine illustrations a second time while she was moving house!
- Richard Kluczynski for taking Tony's cover photo.
- Jill Fairbairns who let Tony know that presenting our story as a fable was not such a stupid idea.
- Jeremy Keeley (and the Sadler Heath organisation) who invited us to use the fable for their members to learn about how they lead and facilitate during change.
- Bob McKenzie and Vicky Costick at Organisations and People Journal who published the fable in its earlier form in their Feb 2008 edition.
- Alex Villar-Hanser who joined with Tony in a study to harvest merger know-how from colleagues in their consultancy network. In particular to Didier Marlier, Tritia Neeb, Michael Newman and Chris Parker who have so generously contributed to Tony's practice over recent years.
- Our families for putting up with us and the book during the period of writing. For Philip: Annette, Yona and Lucas who had to endure the 5am starts and endless mealtime discussions. For Tony: Helen, Wil and Nancy who bring his attention back to them when he is lost in writing. Helen said to Tony after his last book, never again. Perhaps that is why there is a gap of 12 years!

About the authors

Philip Goodwin

Philip has been British Council Regional Director for East and West Africa based in Nairobi, Kenya since May 2004. He joined British Council in 1999 and has undertaken leadership positions for them in Belgium, Pakistan and Uganda. He has previously worked as an aid worker on community development in Timbuktu, Mali and as a policy researcher on environment and aid issues. He met his wife Annette in Mali and today they have two young children.

Philip's leadership motivation is to create teams that are self-confident, capable and passionate about what they do. The puzzle for him in this current project has been how to do this when the teams are so large and spread across such distances. Seeing and hearing the sense of achievement, confidence and enthusiasm for change amongst his team has been an inspiration.

Today, his leadership strength is in managing organisational transformation and building a strong sense of strategic alignment and creativity across large teams. He holds a doctorate in Cultural Geography from the University of London and as a musician and songwriter he also makes albums with his band MoneyShot.

Tony Page

Tony set up 20 years ago as an independent facilitator and coach after dipping his fingers into payment systems, training, organisation design, strategy, branding and market research. Already exposed to people and practices in telecoms, engineering, pharmaceuticals, hospitality, financial services and the public sector, Tony contributed to a challenging series of mergers and change projects.

A happy fruition of this phase was his first book *"Diary of a Change Agent"*, acclaimed for its insightful reflections on how to facilitate, lead and learn through change. Three years ago the African merger launched Tony on a new adventure (his "most exciting project") which raised his game. Inspired by participants' awakening, eyes sparkling, ready to join up and move on, his new focus is "showing leaders how to create leaders and teams, that grip their most difficult challenges".

Tony's reputation with top teams and executive boards in diverse far flung organisations, has been achieved by using the tools outlined here, often alongside Ben Parker or another colleague from his international network. He qualified as a chartered business psychologist, after graduating from Nottingham University (where he met his wife Helen). Having served for six years as a school governor and with his two children now grown up, Tony enjoys his new-found freedom to tramp the globe, cycle, swim, run, read and chat over a drink with friends.

Index